This book delivers a roadmap for students looking to maximize their investment in higher education, offering the tools necessary to stand out among the crowds of eager, young professionals.

—Karim Faris
General Partner, GV (Formerly Google Ventures)

After reading this book, students will know not only what it means to be in the driver's seat of their education and professional careers but also what it looks like to play an active role in their own success.

—Congressman Peter Deutsch
Member of the US House of Representatives (1993–2005)

My assessment of candidates has always been less quantifiable and based more on a gut feeling. Mandee and David have captured and organized the exact qualities that I'm looking for. Better still, they give specific instructions on how to obtain and demonstrate the experience that admissions and talent acquisition professional like me are seeking.

—Debbie Fredberg
Talent Acquisition Manager, Boston Consulting Group
Former Assistant Director of Admissions, Harvard Business School
Former Associate Director of Career Development,
MIT Sloan School of Management

The University and Beyond is the book that I wish I'd had as I was entering college and then embarking upon my own career. Although there are elements of inspiration in it, the book stands out for its practical, actionable advice.
In an increasingly competitive world, *To University and Beyond* will show you how to stand out as you embark upon your career, and it does so in a practical, actionable way.
I've led teams, companies, and organizations for 30 years. How I wish every newly minted college graduate I ever hired would have read *To University and Beyond* and done what Mandee and David recommend! This is by far the most practical guide to help you find early career success.

—Patrick Mullane
Executive Director, Harvard Business School Online

Prospective and current students as well as recent graduates will benefit from *To University and Beyond*. The authors' key insights regarding the innumerable opportunities available to college-aged adults set this book apart as a go-to resource for anyone interested in catapulting themselves into a career.

—Jackie Gordon
Managing Director, Deutsche Bank

Your first job is often the most important indicator of future career opportunity and success. Mandee and David offer great tips and resources to map out a successful future career path for college students.

—Allison O'Kelly
CEO and Founder of Corps Team

Drawing on decades of education and business experience, Adler and Teten provide tomorrow's leaders with an instruction manual for making the most of college.

—Ethan J. Hollander
Professor of Political Science, Wabash College

To University and Beyond clearly explains making the most out of your education in and out of the classroom. The action-oriented tips to start and maintain a successful career provided by the book make it a valuable resource for students and professionals.

—Stephanie L. Carey
PhD, Research Professor
University of South Florida, College of Engineering

Eye-popping college tuition sparks the question from parents and students—"How do I maximize this investment?" Authors Adler and Teten give hundreds of tips and clear directions to guide you through the college years and beyond. A perfect high school graduation gift!

—Eva Bongiovanni
COO of InfoLawGroup and Adjunct Lecturer,
Northwestern University

Pragmatic, logical, helpful, and practical. I wish 20-year-old me would have had access to this book. Mandee and David do an outstanding job sharing their collective wisdom and insights, often including specific details that can certainly help lead to eminent success in one's personal and professional life.

—Terry W. Knaus
Executive Director
Higher Education Consultants Association

To University and Beyond: *Launch Your Career in High Gear*

To University and Beyond: *Launch Your Career in High Gear*

by Mandee Heller Adler and David Teten

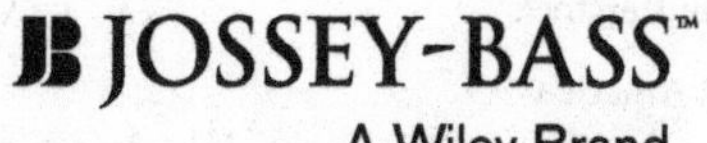

Jossey-Bass
A Wiley Imprint
111 River St, Hoboken, NJ 07030
www.josseybass.com

Jossey-Bass books and products are available through most bookstores. To contact Jossey-Bass directly, call our Customer Care Department within the U.S. at 800–956–7739, outside the U.S. at +1 317 572 3986, or fax +1 317 572 4002.

Wiley also publishes its books in a variety of electronic formats and by print-on-demand. Some material included with standard print versions of this book may not be included in ebooks or in print-on-demand. If this book refers to media such as a CD or DVD that is not included in the version you purchased, you may download this material at http://booksupport.wiley.com. For more information about Wiley products, visit www.wiley.com.

Library of Congress Cataloging-in-Publication Data

Names: Adler, Mandee Heller, author. | Teten, David, author. | Jossey-Bass Inc., publisher.
Title: To university and beyond : launch your career in high gear / by Mandee Heller Adler and David Teten.
Description: First edition. | Hoboken, NJ : Jossey-Bass, 2021.
Identifiers: LCCN 2020055778 (print) | LCCN 2020055779 (ebook) | ISBN 9781119757924 (paperback) | ISBN 9781119758976 (adobe pdf) | ISBN 9781119758983 (epub)
Subjects: LCSH: Career development. | Vocational guidance. | Counseling in higher education.
Classification: LCC HF5381 .A35 2021 (print) | LCC HF5381 (ebook) | DDC 650.1—dc23
LC record available at https://lccn.loc.gov/2020055778
LC ebook record available at https://lccn.loc.gov/2020055779

Cover Design: Wiley
Cover Images: © galacticus/Shutterstock

Printed in the United States of America
FIRST EDITION

SKY10025140_022521

Contents

About the Authors

Mandee Heller Adler is the founder and managing partner of International College Counselors (`InternationalCollegeCounselors.com`) and its subsidiary Edit the Work (`EditTheWork.com`). International College Counselors is one of the world's largest education counseling companies, specializing in exceptionally personalized support for students and their families worldwide who seek acceptance to colleges, graduate schools, and boarding schools in the United States. Since 2004, Mandee and her team of expert college advisors have worked one-on-one with thousands of families to create individualized plans and to get students accepted into dream schools. Edit the Work specializes in writing support, including college admissions essays, resumes, and cover letters, particularly for college students.

Mandee is a graduate of the University of Pennsylvania, where she graduated as a Benjamin Franklin Scholar, with honors and two degrees—one from the Wharton School and one from the College of Arts and Sciences. She also earned her MBA from Harvard Business School, where she was selected as a Class Day Speaker. Additionally, she studied at ICADE, a premier business school located in Madrid, Spain, after receiving a fellowship from Rotary International. Her many community-related activities include serving on the Executive Board of the Penn Fund and volunteering for 13 years as an alumni interviewer for the school. She currently serves as co-president of the Penn Gold Coast Alumni Association.

Mandee authored two books, *From Public School to the Ivy League: How to Get into a Top School Without Top Dollar Resources* and *International Admissions: How to Get Accepted to US Colleges*. She has been featured in dozens of newspapers, magazines, and radio and television programs, including the *New York Times*, the *Wall Street Journal*, *US News and World Report*, *USA Today*, *Fortune*, NBC News, and FOX Business News.

She is a Certified Educational Planner and a member of the Independent Educational Counselors Association (IECA), the National Association of College Admissions Counselors (NACAC), and Higher Education Consultants Association (HECA). Prior to starting International College Counselors, Mandee worked as an investment banker for Goldman, Sachs & Co. in New York. She later cofounded HerDollar, Inc., which she sold to Siebert Financial Corp (NASDAQ: SIEB).

Mandee is a South Florida native, and the middle of three sisters. She is the mother of two remarkable daughters, Rebecca and Sara Pearl, and the wife to an extraordinary husband, Dr. Jason Adler, who she met while playing water polo in college. When not meeting with students, visiting colleges or learning about them, she spends most of her free time reading, losing to her mother at Scrabble, and enjoying Friday night dinners with her extended family.

Please sign up for her mailing list at https://internationalcollegecounselors.com/contact-us and follow her on social media at facebook.com/InternationalCollegeCounselors and twitter.com/College_Experts.

David Teten is CEO of Versatile Venture Capital (`VersatileVC.com`), a New York-based venture capital fund. He has also advised such institutional investors as Birch Hill Equity, Goldman Sachs Special Situations Group, Icahn Enterprises, LLR Partners, Right Side Capital, and OTMT Investments.

David was formerly a managing partner with HOF Capital, an international venture capital fund backed by over 70 families and organizations across 21 countries, and a partner with ff Venture Capital. He particularly focuses on investing in financial technology, sales technology, and education technology.

David is founder of Harvard Business School Alumni Angels of Greater New York, the largest angel group on the East Coast. He was previously a managing director with Evalueserve, a 2,500-person global research and analytics company, and founder and CEO of Circle of Experts, an investment research firm acquired by Evalueserve. He worked with Bear Stearns' Investment Banking division in their technology/defense mergers and acquisitions team. David holds a Harvard MBA (Second Year Honors) and a Yale BA with a double major in Economics and Psychology (with Distinction in the major). While in college, he founded an IT consulting group specializing in serving nonprofits.

David is the author of *The Virtual Handshake: Opening Doors and Closing Deals Online*, and has published research on investment best practices in *Harvard Business Review*, the *Journal of Private Equity*, Institutional Investor, Entrepreneur.com, PE Hub, Techcrunch, and VentureBeat. David is cofounder of PEVCTech.com, an online community focused on helping private equity and venture capital funds make better investments through technology.

He is married and has four children. David grew up in Marin County, Northern California. He trains in parkour and bodyweight exercises. He speaks passable French and Hebrew but has completely lost the Portuguese he learned while working in Brazil.

He founded the "Ambassadors at Large" organization for the 2020 Biden/Harris Presidential campaign.

Please sign up for his mailing list at teten.com, where he writes about entrepreneurship, investing, and life hacks. You can also follow David on social media at:

https://angel.co/p/teten
https://diigo.com/user/dteten
https://linkedin.com/in/teten
https://twitter.com/dteten
https://goodreads.com/user/show/5576313-david-teten
Youtube: https://teten.com/youtube

1 Why We Wrote This Book

David Teten

Partway through Yale, I realized that I was surrounded by kids who had advantages I didn't. They were walking right through doors I didn't even know existed.

All my classmates seemed to have attended elite boarding schools and have parents who worked on Wall Street. Meanwhile, my mother was a choreographer, and my father left school in Paris at age 13 to apprentice in a leather goods factory. I had friends getting internships at Goldman Sachs freshman year; I thought Goldman Sachs sold ladies' handbags.

I had aspirations to have children myself, and I started taking notes on what I was learning about how to "work the system." I wanted my kids to have the systematic understanding that I lacked. As I advanced, I took more notes, planning to eventually publish a book, but waiting for the right time and coauthor. I finally realized that I had known the right coauthor all along: Mandee Heller Adler, a friend who overlapped with me at Harvard Business School.

As I've learned more since Harvard, I realized what skills really matter for the next generation. Seth Masters, former chief investment officer (CIO) of AB (a $500 billion investment management firm), observes that young people have to be ready for an environment where functional skills depreciate rapidly; where the information economy will be dominant; and where few people will spend a career in the same job category . . . let alone the same firm.

You need the skills that you can learn in class: how to absorb information, how to ask questions, how to write well, how to be a good team member, foreign languages, programming languages, etc. But you also need skills you will really learn only in a work setting, even if that work setting is a group of students running a club. For example, how to pitch yourself; how to pitch a product; how to build a team; how to run a team.

We certainly think you should take your classes seriously and get good grades. But for most people, the exact material you study in school is far less important than learning how to learn, given how fast skills get out of date.

When I was a junior in college, I suddenly realized there was a whole world of institutions who wanted to give me money or give me a free education, just because I was a young person. Free stuff? Sign me up!

I literally laced up my sneakers and spent 3 hours jogging to every single academic department at Yale, copying down information from the posters on each department's bulletin boards. As a direct result, that year:

- I entered a writing contest and won a cash prize.
- I won an award from the Yale English department.
- I won a scholarship to spend a week at Mount Holyoke College studying German Studies and Europe.
- I won a scholarship to study political philosophy for a week in the Czech Republic.
- I won a scholarship to spend a long weekend at the US Military Academy (West Point) studying national security issues.

It's not that I was such an amazing candidate. It's just that I applied. Most of my peers were unaware of these opportunities.

We'll save you the jog. We have listed in this book all of the most selective generalist programs we have found and also how to find the niche programs relevant to your particular major and situation. Almost all of these programs are free or highly subsidized, and some are not as competitive as you may think. Taking summer classes is great, but you may get even more value from some of the programs we list.

The opportunities we list not only expose you to new disciplines and parts of the world, but they also look amazing on resumes and graduate school applications! We also list programs focused on young professionals, as opposed to current students. We think it's helpful to have on your radar programs that are relevant for your future self, not just your current self.

One of the reasons people pay so much to attend university is the breadth of the alumni base. But over time I realized that you can meet great people regardless of where you went to school . . . if you put yourself in other, equally challenging environments. The programs we list are not graduate schools, but they are the functional equivalent of the Ivy League. And what's more, they are often easier to get into because fewer people know about them.

When we were near the finish line of writing this book, suddenly the COVID-19 pandemic hit globally. This disruptive crisis is making both companies and people rethink the value of formal, in-person, traditional education. For hundreds of years, most people thought that it was mandatory to live in close proximity with other young adults to get an education. Now people realize that's not necessarily the case.

I'll share another reason I wrote this book: Just like your parents, I have a lot of advice I'd like my kids to follow. And you, like most young people, sometimes don't want to follow your parents' counsel. But one trick I've learned in raising four kids: if good advice comes from anywhere OTHER than my wife and me, my kids are far more likely to pay attention. So, I'm going to give this book to my kids. Because it looks official with a pretty cover, they're far more likely to heed it.

Your early career years are like the initial financing round for a start-up company. If you don't hit your key milestones during the critical age 18–23 time period, the next stages get increasingly more difficult.

The core theme of Atul Gawande's book *The Checklist Manifesto* is:

- Checklists improve performance, even saving lives, but . . .
- Most people resist using checklists.

I agree with both of these points. Our goal here is to create a set of checklists for your life in school, as well as in your early career.

Mandee Heller Adler

After working on Wall Street, selling an Internet company, and then running a division of a publicly traded company, I was ready for a new challenge. I wanted a career with meaning, and to use my blessings to help others. To quote Benjamin Franklin, I wanted to "do well by doing good." I realized that so much of what I had accomplished up to that point was due to advantages I received through higher education, first at the University of Pennsylvania and then later at Harvard Business School. This led me to independent college counseling: I would help other students to reach their academic goals.

Over time, my mission became International College Counselors, a global education advising business with students in 13 countries and counselors across the United States. When I was approached by David to help turn this book into reality, I realized that although I was very good at helping my students get into a top college, what they really needed next was a road map to best take advantage of the opportunities they were being given. This book is the answer. It's great to go to Stanford, but not if you graduate unemployed and without allies. This book will help young adults make the most of their early career years, so that they can maximize their investments of time and money, and become confident and successful citizens. I thank you for reading!

Mandee and David

You're likely investing a lot of money, and a lot of time, to get yourself educated. We definitely did. How can you maximize the benefits of all the years and all the money that you are investing?

To prepare this book, we interviewed dozens of professionals who work with young people early in their career, as well as our classmates from the University of Pennsylvania, Yale University, and Harvard Business School and clients of International College Counselors. We asked what were the most effective uses of their time during their education and also probed to learn about what were the least effective uses of their time.

We hope you get a lot of value from our book! Please don't hesitate to contact us via `InternationalCollegeCounselors.com` and `Teten.com`.

College Is Not for Everyone: Get Paid to Learn

We realize you'll most likely get a traditional undergraduate degree and maybe more degrees beyond that. That said, a traditional degree is not the right choice for everyone. It can be expensive, time consuming, and may leave you with a mountain of debt. Of course, it's also a credential and network you can use for the rest of your life.

Before you and your family make an expensive long-term commitment, we encourage you to consider some other options that may pay you immediately, may be more prestigious, and are likely much faster. We think that regardless of what path you take, the ideas we discuss in this book are going to help you take maximum advantage of whatever road is right for you.

We've ranked in this chapter some educational options for you, roughly in declining order of how much money you can get paid. "Much better that someone pays you, than you pay tuition to someone else, right?"

An exceptional, and very competitive, option is the Thiel Fellowship (`thielfellowship.org`). "The Thiel Fellowship is a two-year program for young people [under age 22] who want to build new things. Thiel Fellows skip or step out of college to receive a $100,000 grant and support from the Thiel Foundation's network of founders, investors, and scientists."

Another option is the technology accelerators, that is, Y Combinator (`ycombinator.com`) and TechStars (`Techstars.com`). These will give you capital (typically $100,000–$200,000) to build a new company, and you can pay yourself a salary out of that capital. You need to have an idea and typically a prototype before they'll accept you. You'll graduate as chief executive officer (CEO) of a funded start-up company.

An emerging category of accelerator is the "Talent Investors." These typically provide many of the services you would see in an accelerator: mentorship, office space, investment into the company. However, Talent

Investors fund individuals, rather than companies. They typically pay you a modest stipend (e.g. $2,000/month) for several months to research a start-up idea. Leaders include Antler (antler.co) and Entrepreneur First (joinef.com).

Military training teaches you real-world skills that you'll never get in a traditional college, and in certain roles you'll work with sophisticated technologies that typical universities cannot afford. See https://usa.gov/join-military and https://military.com/join-armed-forces.

Another option is targeted education programs that are squarely focused on career preparation and dispense with most of the traditional overhead of universities. These are typically far cheaper than a conventional university. Some examples:

- HackerU (hackerusa.com) collaborates with top tier universities to provide immersive, comprehensive, and rigorous programs in digital skills, with salaries ranging from $50,000 to $100,000.
- Lambda School (lambdaschool.com) teaches the tech skills you need to launch a new career in just 9 months. You don't pay tuition until you land a job making at least $50,000 a year.
- Praxis (discoverpraxis.com) says, "During . . . . bootcamp you'll learn the skills employers are looking for as well as how to showcase those skills, and then you'll put them to use during your apprenticeship while getting paid. During the apprenticeship you'll make a minimum of $15,000, and the average salary upon graduation for Praxis grads is $50,000/year." Tuition: $12,000.
- Revature (revature.com) teaches coding at no cost and then helps you find a job.

For an overview of coding bootcamps, see Coursereport.com. If you want to borrow money for this purpose, you may find ClimbCredit.com helpful. Forte (forteofficial.com)[1] finances vocational reskilling at no cost to either students or governments.

The last option is to simply teach yourself. Famed writer Ray Bradbury said,

> *I didn't go to college, but when I graduated from high school I went down to the local library and I spent ten years there, two or three days a week, and I got a better education than most people get from universities. So I graduated from the library when I was twenty-eight years old.*[2]

Bradbury did this long before the Internet. Now you can teach yourself almost any skill online, for free. This does take a high level of self-control and motivation. If you take the autodidact path, it will typically be challenging to get your first paid job, because you'll be lacking traditional credentials. However, once you're employed and do well in your job, your lack of traditional credentials will matter much less.

On almost any subject imaginable, you can find newsletters, podcasts, videos, and books. You'll find very influential people are sometimes surprisingly approachable on social media, if you engage thoughtfully with them. TheForage.com offers free virtual work experience from leading companies such as Deloitte, KPMG, and more.

The simplest way to learn a subject online is via a MOOC (Massive Open Online Course). Many offer professional certificates, and some offer courses in conjunction with traditional colleges. Businesses offering classes include Disney, Goldman Sachs, IBM, and The Linux Foundation. Courses are typically free unless a student intends to obtain recognized credit, such as a degree or certification.

We've listed here the major MOOCs:

- Coursera (coursera.org)
- EdX (edx.org)
- FutureLearn (futurelearn.com)
- Khan Academy (khanacademy.org)
- MIT OpencourseWare (ocw.mit.edu)
- Open Education (sparcopen.org/open-education)
- OpenLearn (open.edu/openlearn)
- On Deck (https://www.beondeck.com/)

Before Your First Class

Good news for many of you: attending a highly selective college does not correlate with greater satisfaction, according to the Strada-Gallup College Student Survey.[3] What does make people more satisfied includes "establishing a deep connection with a mentor, taking on a sustained academic project, and playing a significant part in a campus organization." In other words, don't just eat your education like a customer in a restaurant (passively); go into the kitchen and season it the way you like it.

David Alworth, a research associate in the Center for Business and Government at the Harvard Kennedy School, said,

> *You should think about your time in school as time that you are intentionally shaping, directing, and producing. During seminar classes, for example, you should feel both obligated and privileged to help steer the discussion with your peers and your instructor. In large lecture classes, you might help organize a smaller reading or study group.*

One of the first things you will notice when you get accepted to an educational program is that the accepted students immediately start to connect with each other on social media. Your school will often create regional get-togethers, which often continue through student planning well throughout the summer, as well as specialized online groups, for example, a Facebook or LinkedIn group for your class.

We recommend that you sign up for all of the online groups for your class and institution. These are wonderful opportunities to get to know your classmates and to ease your transition into your new educational home. Many of the friendships you make during the early months are the friendships you will retain for a lifetime.

Prepare a 30-second "elevator pitch" answer to the two most commonly asked questions you will get: (i) Where are you from? (ii) What is your major? Of course, you can answer these questions with simple answers like "Marin County" or "math," or you can choose to provide insight into who you are and what you hope to get out of your education. You can also use your answers to learn more about your classmates. Perhaps try something like: "I am from Miami, and I love filmmaking and water sports. Where are you from? What clubs are you interested in?" And, for the major, try, "I hope to major in math because I plan to enter sports analytics after graduation. How about you?"

Or, for students entering graduate school, be prepared to answer these questions:

- What did you do before coming to school?
- What are you planning to do after school?

People love when you ask them questions. Two thoughtful conversations are far more valuable than a dozen forgettable interactions.

Write very carefully your entry in the class directory and in any other social media systems used by your peers. Professors often refer to these sources to get to know their students prior to courses; this is the first impression you will make. A lot of people will search in these directories for students who share their interests, for example, students who wrote "Jewish," "Chinese," or "environment" in their profiles. Make sure that your entries use keywords that people might use in looking for people like you.

Set up and manage one central hub for your online presence. Whenever you introduce yourself online, point to that platform. This way people can follow up with you, without being restricted by the platform where you met.

The ideal online presence is a personal website, for example `teten.com`. An option with less flexibility is to build your profile using a service like `About.me` or `Wix.com`. The last option is to use a platform like LinkedIn. However, any individual social media platform like LinkedIn places restrictions on your online presence. It's much safer to set up a neutral venue. Don't build on someone else's platform; build on your own.

Mandee: We encourage our International College Counselors students as young as high school to start setting up LinkedIn accounts for personal information and websites, Facebook or Instagram accounts for a business or organization that the teen started or runs. This puts our students "on the digital map," and allows them to create a carefully cultivated presence online. A professional LinkedIn page for a motivated high school, college, or graduate student is both acceptable and well regarded. By having social media accounts at a young age, you can also start to cultivate your network. Adding new friends or professional contacts to your social media platforms ensures that you don't lose track of them over the years, and you can easily reach out for future communications.

When you introduce yourself online, try to include the major points that you'd cover in the first 10 minutes of an introductory conversation with a new friend. It's common that in an online class or community, the moderator may ask everyone to introduce themselves. Make sure to highlight anything memorable or unusual about yourself, as it's hard to differentiate when everyone is in a sea of the same font. Include a photo if possible.

Also, include as many points of common interests as possible because each of them can be a conversation starter. For example, list the cities you've lived in, languages you speak, hobbies, something unusual about your family or background, pets. If the medium allows for hashtags (e.g. in Slack), we recommend hashtagging your hobbies, intended career field, and major. Limit your hashtags to four to six items.

Here are sample self-introduction from two college students:

> Hi everyone! My name is Nicole [Odzer]. I was born and raised in Miami, FL, and I am currently a rising senior at Yale University. I am majoring in Molecular, Cellular, and Developmental Biology, and I hope to attend medical school after graduating. I love biology and have been conducting research in a molecular biology lab at Yale since my sophomore year, focusing on the study of large non-coding RNAs! The rest of my free time in school is spent volunteering and shadowing at the hospital, playing viola in a student orchestra, and singing in a student-run a cappella group! Some fun facts about me are that I have travelled to over 30 national parks and monuments in the United States (my family really loves hiking), and that I scuba dive!

> Hi all, I'm Michael [Waldman]. I was born in Buenos Aires but moved to the US at age 4, and to Chicago at 18 to study Computer Science and Engineering at Northwestern University. The past few summers, I've been immersed in the tech industry, and have gotten the chance to work at Facebook, and now Instagram as a software engineer. I also enjoy hobby projects in computer science and tinkering with electronics. Besides all the coding I do, I really enjoy bike riding, boxing, good comedies, mentoring and spending time with my family. A fun fact about me is these days, I do most of my work on a walking desk (a standing desk with a treadmill under), and in the past 6 months working from home I've logged over 1,500 miles.

Here are two examples from MBAs at Massachusetts Institute of Technology's Sloan School of Management:

> Hi everyone! My name is Katherine Boe Heuck, but please call me Kate. I currently live in Washington, DC, where I also grew up. I graduated from Washington and Lee University in 2013 and majored in Chinese and Biology. After college, I worked and lived in Hebei Province and Shanghai, China, for 5 years, in sustainability consulting for the Joint US-China Collaboration on Clean Energy. I worked with food & beverage and consumer packaged goods companies, specifically Danone and Alibaba HeMa (cashless grocery store), which were looking to sustainably innovate products and brands for the urban Chinese market. I also ran my own education company before coming to Sloan. I speak fluent Mandarin and I plan to stay connected to Greater China throughout my career, although most likely based in the US. I want to pursue a career in #VentureCapital, focusing on #edtech. I'm also interested in getting involved with the #sustainability conference and the impact investing club. This summer, I'm interning with Versatile Venture Capital. My hobbies include #sailing, #golf, and #reading historical non-fiction. My husband Sam Heuck is also in our MBA class and we are looking forward to meeting you all. Please reach out if we share interests! My personal email is kate@heuck.com and my school email is kbheuck@mit.edu. You can find me online at `https://linkedin.com/in/katherine-boe/`.

> Hey Sloanies! My name is Sam Heuck. My wife Kate Boe Heuck and I are excited to join the class of 2022. I currently live in Washington, DC, but my hometown is Pittsburgh. I graduated from Kenyon College in 2012 with a degree in Political Science and Chinese. I speak Mandarin fluently and spent 6 years in Shanghai, China working in management in textiles manufacturing companies. Post-MBA, I hope to join a private equity fund, continuing to focus on #manufacturing and industrial and #supply chain technology. I'm also interested in emerging markets, having worked and travelled in China, India, and Vietnam. My hobbies include #sailing, #squash, #travel, and #reading. This summer, I am interning for Schematic Ventures, an early-stage venture capital fund that focuses on industrial technologies based in San Francisco. My email address is sam@heuck.com and my school email is sdheuck@mit.edu. I look forward to meeting you all and connecting. You can find me online at `https://linkedin.com/in/sam-heuck-80a56558/`.

Upgrade your wardrobe. Seriously. If you can afford it—prepare for a more mature stage in your life. Do you have a nice suit for job interviews? How about a clean pair of jeans and a collared shirt for meetings with professors? Although you don't need to lose your identity, do dress to show you care, especially when dealing with faculty and employers. Consider some of the online services that make it easy to dress professionally, for example, `Poshmark.com` or `Renttherunway.com`.

Read through and familiarize yourself with the main sections of the school intranet. Learn about where important school news is posted. You don't want to be well into the first semester before you learn about the many wonderful speakers and events you've missed. A great habit is to review the school public calendar once a week to see which businesspeople, politicians, academics, or other interesting people are visiting the campus.

If you can, find an older classmate who can help guide you: course choices, club activities, and the unwritten rules. If you can't find a current student, contact an alumni organization, and see if there is a recent graduate who can speak with you. Some schools will designate a "Big Sib" to smooth your process. The extracurricular clubs are a great way to meet friendly students with more experience than you.

Contact the presidents of the clubs you are interested in. Join clubs from the very beginning to see if you are in the right place, or if you need to seek other opportunities for learning. The earlier you get involved, the more easily you can switch directions or take a leadership role in a club you enjoy. Unlike high school, there will be no "free periods" for clubs. Getting on a club mailing list is free; you can decide whether or not you want to participate in a given club once you get a sense of their activities.

4 Who Do You Know? Who Knows You?

The whole value of the dime is in knowing what to do with it.
—*Ralph Waldo Emerson*

As a structure for this chapter, we're going to use the "Seven Keys" to understanding the value of your community around you—who knows you, and whom you know. Creating a community of friends and supporters is critical to your professional advancement, especially in the business world.

Our book may seem overly focused on building a supportive community, that is, a network. That's only because we think that the topic is insufficiently covered in traditional curricula about success. *Please don't mistake the disproportionate coverage for the relative importance of who knows you and who you know. Your character and competence are most important in driving your success*, and that's why we list them first in the following framework.

Reid Hoffman, cofounder of LinkedIn, wrote in "My 2020 Vision for Graduates: How to Be Optimistic in Terrible Times":[4]

> *Your superpower at the moment: . . . [A]s a person who is most likely in their 20s, you're at a more adaptive point in your life than those who are both younger and older than you.*
>
> *Behind every new breakthrough technology, every new industry trend, there are people. That's where everything starts. And while knowledge creates awareness—you might know that company X is growing fast because you read about it in the news—relationships create opportunities.*

Figure out ways to put yourself near the hubs of the networks that matter most in your given career domain.

The right group of friends is like your own proprietary board of directors.

Let's use a simple example. We'll assume that you are a student living in San Francisco, and you have a network of three people: Armand, Brenda, and Chaim.

What exactly is the value of your community?[5]

Patrick Mullane, a graduate of the University of Notre Dame, Harvard Business School, and currently the executive director of HBS Online (Harvard Business School), writes:

Working in an academic institution now has driven home to me how valuable a connection to a faculty member can be. Of course, you can learn from them. But more importantly, they will likely have connections in a discipline or an industry that can help you in a myriad of ways. This has been the biggest lesson of my life: networks matter. They matter a lot. In fact, they matter so much that I think it should be one of the principal things seniors consider when choosing their educational path. Does the school have a strong network in a region where I want to live or in a discipline I want to study? These are important things to consider among a host of other factors, but I'd still rank the "network strength" of a school as one of the top two or three things. And networking in a big way starts early: first with your classmates and next with your faculty.

When you're researching a school, consider asking: What percentage of alumni come to reunions? What percentage donate to the institution? What is the school's Net Promoter Score? (NPS is a popular measure of an institution's customer satisfaction levels.)

Seven Keys drive the value of your community:

1. your **Character**	Armand and Chaim all think of you as a trustworthy, high-Character person. However, you have been late for a number of lunch dates with Brenda, and tend to gossip about various common friends with her. As a result, she thinks of you as somewhat unreliable and of more mediocre Character.
2. your **Competence**	Armand, Brenda, and Chaim all know that you are an excellent, ambitious student. You have perceived high Competence as a student, which extends to perceived high Competence in your chosen field.
3. Relevance of the people you know	Armand and Brenda work for ExxonMobil Corporation, a multinational company that is a potential summer employer. They are high Relevance. Chaim is an unpublished fiction writer, so he is low Relevance as a potential employer.
4. the **Information** you have about your network	You have current work and home contact Information for Armand, Brenda, and Chaim. In addition, because you see Armand and Chaim so often, you have current Information about their mood, how happy they are in their job, and all sorts of other useful background Information.
5. Strength of your relationships	You overlapped in high school with Armand and Chaim and have been close friends with them since then. You go out occasionally for dinner, so you have a high Strength relationship with them. You see Brenda only about twice a year; that relationship is low Strength.
6. Number of people in your network	You only have four dozen people in your network, so you have a very low Number.
7. Diversity	Armand, Brenda, and Chaim are all of a different religion and cultural background than you, and they all work in a different industry than you. However, the three also all live in the Bay Area, so they are not diverse geographically. On the whole, you have a modest level of Diversity.

We've just used the Seven Keys to analyze your network. To define these terms more formally, we will explain them using two people: "You" (the center of the network) and "Acquaintance" (which could be your friend, neighbor, coworker, or any other person you know).

Five of the keys measure the relationship between you and your Acquaintance:

***Character*—Your integrity, clarity of motives, consistency of behavior, openness, discretion, and trustworthiness.** This is driven by both the real content of your Character and by what each Acquaintance views as your Character.

***Competence*—Your ability to "walk your talk" and do well the job that you claim to be able to do, your demonstrated credentials and capability.** It includes task-specific knowledge and skills, interpersonal skills, business sense, and judgment. This is driven by both the real level of your Competence and by what each Acquaintance views as the level of your Competence.

***Relevance*—The Acquaintance's value to you,** defined as the Acquaintance's ability to contribute to your specific goals. The Acquaintance's Relevance is typically driven by the value of the Acquaintance's *own* network.

***Information*—The data that you have about the Acquaintance.** First are the basic coordinates: email, phone numbers, home phone, family Information, social media IDs, etc. Also invaluable is Information about professional background, where they are in their career, his likes and dislikes, etc.

***Strength*—The closeness of the relationship between you and your Acquaintance.** This reflects how much time you spend together, the length of the relationship, and the degree of trust and reciprocity in your relationship.

The sixth key measures the number of people in your community:

***Number*—How many people you know directly.** Anthropologist Robin Dunbar popularized the idea that most people can really maintain only about 150 connections at once. Now that everyone is on social media, we believe that you can maintain shallow connections with a much larger number of people. As a benchmark, we suggest that you graduate from college with a core "friend group" that might fit around one dinner table, and a larger "tribe" which might be perhaps 20 to 150 people. Not coincidentally, that's roughly the typical size of the core members of a fraternity, sports team, or active club.

Lastly, the seventh key measures the diversity of your community:

***Diversity*—Heterogeneity of your network**, by geography, profession, hierarchical position, and industry. In addition, your network should ideally be Diverse by age, sex, ethnicity, tenure, socioeconomic status, sexual orientation, and so on.

For the mathematically inclined, we can use a formula to summarize this:

Ch = Character

Co = Competence

R = Relevance

I = Information

S = Strength

N = Number

D = Diversity

$$\textbf{Network Value} = D * \sum_{n=1}^{N} \left(Ch_n * Co_n * R_n * I_n * S_n \right)$$

For the non-math majors reading this book, the $\sum$ sign means "summation" of all of the values in parentheses, for each of the people in your network.

As an absolute rule, credibility—your Character and your Competence—must underlie your network. A massive network will not aid you if you are selling an inferior product or trying to get a job for which you are unqualified. In fact, such a network will rapidly become a liability, as too many people will be aware of the inferior goods you are peddling. No matter how much your friends like you, they will not recommend you for a job if they believe that you are unethical, tardy, sloppy, or otherwise act unprofessionally.

The ideal network has a large Number of Diverse people who think highly of you and with whom you are well bonded. This principle explains the value of "Outward Bound" expeditions, Ropes Courses, and other similar programs. These retreats all promote quick bonding between participants, that is, fast-action Strength.

Now that we have outlined the Seven Keys, let's discuss some ideas on how to increase the value of each component of your network.

Character

Think long term. A really simple rubric for making good decisions: think through the long-term implications of each decision you make. What happens to you long term if you try that interesting-sounding party drug, or hitting the snooze button instead of going to 8 a.m. lectures.

Guard your reputation. Your knowledge, skills, intellectual agility, and good looks all fade over time, but your reputation stays with you for a lifetime. Do not allow even the appearance of lying or breaking the law. Do not even make jokes about breaking the law (e.g. jokes about flouting environmental laws to make more money.) Your humor indicates what is on your mind. Perception is reality.

If you use drugs and alcohol, do so sparingly. Are you known for being a party animal, or someone with self-control over their use of mind-altering substances?

Play it straight. Cheating is especially common in school, including the use of extra time when not warranted. The faculty may not have noticed, but your peers will not forget. Would you invest in a company led by someone you know who cheated the system? How do you want to be remembered?

Most of your future relationships come from your past relationships, so how people perceive your character can make or break your business. No one wants to work with someone they remember as being dishonest or unintelligent. It is always a bad idea to cheat, both because it's wrong and you might get caught by your professors, but you should be equally worried about being caught by your peers. Those peers who see you cheat might not turn you in, and might not even take it seriously today. But we guarantee that they will remember your ethics when they are considering working with you in the future. Not to mention, most school Honor Codes require students to turn in others whom they observe cheating.

Jack Henry Kapp, real estate executive and Cornell graduate, observes:

> *School taught me that no matter what field or industry I would ultimately enter, success would come from building relationships with people and always maintaining the highest*

level of ethics and honesty in all of my actions. Now that I am in the business world, I realize how important my reputation has been to my success. People tend to work with those they can trust, even if that trust was established at 17 or 18 years old. (personal communication)

Listen much more than you talk. This is why you have two ears and one mouth. You are surrounded by people who know more than you do.

Be humble. An ego is the fastest-growing thing on earth. Don't believe the hype: a degree from a top school is great, but you do not walk on water, you are not smarter than your parents, and even if you get a great job with Google after graduation, that does not imply any guarantees about your long-term success. There are multiple types of intelligences. Maybe you went to a famous school, but your colleague who went to work at age 18 full time and attended community college is more empathetic, stronger at sales, and quicker at adopting new technology. She'll get promoted before you.

Keep your family ties strong. You will not stay in touch with most of the people you meet while a young adult, but your family is forever.

Err on the conservative side in your posting. Although it may be tempting to do so, avoid silly photos with funky hats or glasses or photos showing skin, drugs, and/or alcohol. These photos may seem fun right now, but they may not look so funny in 20 years. In 2017, Harvard rescinded offers to 10 high school students who posted offensive memes in a Facebook group. Harvard did the same in 2019 to a senior from the Marjory Stoneman Douglas High School in Parkland, Florida, who had used offensive language at age 16. Students have also been asked to leave colleges solely because of inappropriate online postings. Nothing is private and whatever you put on the Internet is forever.

Competence

Make the most of your time in the classroom. Always attend class and develop solid study habits; for example, for closed-book tests, make flashcards to drill home the key material. For open-book tests, prepare a document that synthesizes the core lessons/tools. For case classes, prepare the case yourself and don't rely on the easy and inferior crutch of study group notes.

Sit in front of the class. It's a great way to stay focused. Often in large auditorium style classrooms, the back of the room will be noisy and filled with the students who are, well, less studious. Sitting in the front ensures that you are surrounded by serious students and that you can see and hear what's going on. We discuss later how to get the most out of virtual classes.

Learn to touch type. The easiest, cheapest step you can take to make your schoolwork dramatically easier is to become a fast typist.

Master the standard office productivity tools. Your competence in personal productivity skills is surprisingly impactful to your efficacy. Most commonly, this includes the G Suite by Google and the Microsoft Office Suite (Word, Excel, and PowerPoint). In a modern workplace, other very leverageable skills include knowing Python, building simple websites, writing blogs, and making YouTube videos.

Prepare text and spreadsheet templates with the format of the response neatly prepared for the assignments you normally get in school. For example, if you are studying history, create a template formatted timeline. If you are required to write a "persuasive essay," create a skeleton with your teacher's recommended sections of such an essay.

Review technology tools that can help you learn more, faster. `SuperMemo.com` helps you remember "everything you'll ever learn" by optimizing intervals between repetition. Anki (`ankiapp.com`) "is a program which makes remembering things easy. Because it's a lot more efficient than traditional study methods, you can either greatly decrease your time spent studying, or greatly increase the amount you learn."

Prepare all your notes for easy skimming to prompt you for ideas. You will almost never have time to access the raw materials during an exam. Ideally, your notes are segmented with clear section titles, and all stored in a searchable directory.

As always, make sure you answer the question that was asked. This is one of the easiest ways to get better grades. Don't answer the question you want to answer; always reread the original assignment before turning in your paper.

Stay abreast of current events. We suggest reading a weekly news magazine, for example, *The Economist* or the Sunday *New York Times*. Avoid receiving only news that falls too far to the left or right. You may not agree with your friends on all issues, but at least you can understand them when they're getting their news from a different political perspective than yours. Remember that by reading your news through social media services, you are usually getting only information that the service feels you will "like." You're in a "filter bubble." Knowing nothing about the other side of an issue can be as detrimental as not knowing anything at all.

If you quote books, magazines, etc., give credit to whom you're quoting. This shows intellectual honesty and respect and also avoids any questions of plagiarism.

When applicable, learn to use graphs and visual aids. One of the reasons why strategy consulting is a feeder to senior executive roles is that consultants develop the ability to communicate complex concepts visually. Yale Professor Emeritus Edward Tufte is the leading expert on this topic; we recommend reading all and any of his books. His most influential book is *The Visual Display of Quantitative Information.*

Learn to speak properly and crisply, using good grammar. Do not say "uh," "um," "ah," "literally," or the many other non-words that pepper the typical conversation. If you want to scare yourself, tape record yourself on an important phone call. Most people who do this are concerned about how erratic the conversation sounds—how it is potholed by conversation-stoppers like "eh" and "you know."

Post reality-based content. If you are going to post an article, be sure that it is from a reputable media source. Posting "fake news" makes you seem unintelligent and lazy and can lead to dangerous misunderstandings about what's really going on in the world. Likewise, if you post content that is inflammatory, you will be shrinking your network and likely hurting society's ability to function. Although you may feel a moral obligation to post your view on certain issues, remember that you will never change someone's mind by being offensive or demeaning. If you want to have a discussion with someone about a sensitive issue, consider private messaging or even a phone call. You're more likely to accomplish your goal effectively.

It is extremely helpful to gain a reputation as a hard worker and an "expert witness" in the first few weeks of class. Once you have done that, the rest of the semester is much easier. Prepare very thoroughly in the first few weeks of class.

Jennifer Stein Simms, University of Pennsylvania graduate and an instructor of marketing strategy via UCLA Extension, observes:

> *As an instructor at UCLA, I was appalled at how many of my students came to class not having read the material or showed an interest in what was being discussed. It was*

almost as if they felt that "class participation" simply meant sitting in a chair in the class for the length of class. CLASS PARTICPATION MEANS PARTICIPATING IN CLASS! That means, coming to class prepared, asking questions, showing an interest. Remember your professors and TAs are paying attention—don't think they don't notice when you are texting or online in class!! You want them to see that you care! (personal communication)

Do not speak unless you have thought out your position thoroughly; are prepared to defend it; and consider it a unique, non-obvious, point. Most of your classmates will assume that a given student is intelligent and well prepared—until you say something that demonstrates otherwise.

Ask a *kushiyah*. Nechama Leibowitz, a prominent Old Testament scholar, emphasized the difference between a question and a *kushiyah*. (This is a Hebrew word without an English equivalent.) A question is a request for information, for example, "When did the first COVID-19 deaths occur in the USA and South Korea?" (Answer: the same date.) A *kushiyah* is the result of a sense of difficulty or problem, based on an understanding of the information: "I noticed that the USA had dramatically more COVID-19 cases and deaths than South Korea, despite having only about six times the population. Why the disparity?" When you ask a *kushiyah*, both the discussion leader and other students will recognize they're working with someone who is smarter than the average, who's absorbing the information and taking the next step to probe.

Leverage your academic work for your long-term career interests. The most impactful papers you will write are (i) publishable in a reputable medium for your industry; (ii) written as a field study for a company you would like to join; (iii) a business plan for a company you want to start; or (iv) a combination of the first three. Likewise, use projects as a way to meet people in your class and to build skill sets you don't already have. With a reputable school as your platform, do not waste your time with mediocre works that go into the professor's hands and shortly thereafter the trash.

David: Here are some examples of students multipurposing their work:

- In 2011–13, I worked with a team of three Columbia MBAs (McKinsey and BCG consultants) on a field study we cowrote on *Best Practices of Venture Capitalists in Increasing the Value of*

Portfolio Companies. They earned an A, and the article was the most-viewed study in the *Journal of Private Equity* for the year following its publication. (See teten.com/pa.)

- One of my HBS classmates did a field study with famed entrepreneur Richard Branson. The field study (a business plan) resulted in him winning an amazing job offer as personal assistant to Richard Branson.
- Two other classmates did a field study that consisted of organizing the Harvard Business School Cyberposium, HBS's annual technology conference. They simultaneously received academic credit, strengthened their resume, and built their network with technology industry leaders.
- A group of classmates wrote a business plan for a start-up, Zefer. Leveraging the intellectual capital available to them on campus, they won the school's Business Plan contest, raised $2 million in venture capital, and started a company. Within a year, they had raised an additional $100 million in committed capital for the company.

Aaron Buxbaum, a senior tech executive and graduate of Georgia Institute of Technology, observes:

> *If you can get collaborative practice actually working out problems and building things, you have a huge advantage going into the actual industry. In addition, it validates your dedication to the job: if you can't stand hanging out with all of the most dedicated people to your concentration now, it's unlikely you'll want to when you're working full time. (personal communication)*

Get some sleep. An extremely common error that students make is to shortchange their sleep. But if you do that, you're not going to learn as well; you'll hurt your long-term health; and you're more prone to depression. It's tempting to stay out late, especially on weekends, but making a fixed commitment to go to bed every night by midnight (or whatever your target is) will serve you well.

Relevance

Connect with the other people in your educational program, not just your immediate classmates. Spend some time with the students in the years above you, faculty, guest speakers, Executive Education students, etc. Executive Education is the umbrella term for educational programming for working professionals, sometimes without a degree. Often, you can get the resume book for Executive Education sessions if you ask your school. These are a gold mine; you can read through it and reach out to people who look like the person you want to become in 15 years. The Executive Education students are essentially on vacation, so they are usually in a good mood, flexible, and happy to meet with students.

David: One of my friends attended a reception for MBAs to meet Harvard Business School Executive Education students on campus, while he was himself just an MBA. The friend met the chief executive officer (CEO) of a midsize company, who ended up offering him a job as his chief of staff. He took the job, and one of the first things he told his new boss: "Hiring people you randomly meet at receptions is definitely not the optimal way to recruit great talent. Let's put in place a more rigorous and standardized recruiting process."

Nadine (Goldberg) Epstein, MSEd, Robertson Scholar at Duke ('16) and currently an assistant director at the Life Design Lab at Johns Hopkins University, said:

> *One of the most impactful things I did early in my career was building relationships with people [on campus] excelling in careers I thought I might want to pursue. Once I started thinking about a career in Higher Education Administration, I emailed folks working in different offices at my own university to ask whether I could meet and learn about their experiences breaking into and working in the field. Each conversation helped me find more and more clarity about where I could see myself working one day; some conversations resulted in a referral to someone else who would eventually offer me an internship or research position; and a few even launched long-term mentorship relationships. To this day, I stay in touch with one of the mentors I met this way during my sophomore year, and we make it a point to catch up anytime we wind up in the same city.*
>
> *I was nervous to send these cold emails at first—would the recipients laugh at me for thinking they'd give up their valuable time to speak with a 19-year-old? Once I swallowed my nerves and hit "send," however, I quickly learned that*

people really enjoy sharing their experiences and advice with students, particularly if they're somehow affiliated with the same university. It's a win-win situation! (personal communication)

Organize student–faculty events. For example, organize a dinner or online meeting in which all of the students in a certain class host the professor and his/her family to a meal.

David: While in grad school, I was co-president of the Jewish Students Association. I organized periodic dinners with professors and visiting business leaders to meet members of the club. These were often joint events, for example, I would invite a prominent real estate investor and the event would be joint-sponsored between my group and the Real Estate Association. This had the benefit both of attracting more people to the event and helping both groups in their recruiting. I also wrote occasionally for the school newspaper throughout my education and used that as an excuse to meet and interview some really interesting and professionally relevant people, including the CEO of the Harvard endowment.

If you're in a study group or a group project, choose members carefully. When former Massachusetts governor Mitt Romney was at Harvard Business School, he recruited some of the most distinguished students in the class for his study group. "He and I said, hey, let's handpick some superstars," said Howard Serkin, a classmate. "He wanted to make straight A's . . . He wanted our study group to be No. 1." Sometimes Mr. Romney arrived early to run his numbers a few extra times. And if his partners were not prepared, "he was not afraid of saying: 'You're letting us down. We want to be the best,'" Mr. Serkin added.[6]

Information

Keep track of who you know. Enter new acquaintances into your online contacts, or if you really want to be organized, register for a contact relationship management (CRM) system (e.g. `Copper.com`, `Salesforce.com`, `Hubspot.com`), and keep it up to date. The exercise of building a database of everyone you know will facilitate keeping in touch with them. But you can't leverage that unique asset without keeping track of what your classmates are doing. We suggest tracking in the CRM where you met someone, to help you recall them later.

David: One of my standard interview questions for salespeople or anyone in an outward-facing job is, "What system do you use to track the contact information for people you meet? How many people are in it?" I ask this question even of undergrads. A mediocre answer, but a typical answer, is, "My phone, and I have a few dozen people's phone numbers in there." A decent answer is "My phone, and I have systematically labeled everyone in the database with how I know them, and what category they're in: investor, potential employer, classmate, etc." An "A+" answer is: "I use a professional Contact Relationship Management (CRM) system. I also use `Contactsplus.com` to pull data from business cards into my personal contact database."

Seek out and get to know your academic advisor. Most schools assign academic advisors for students who are there to help you identify your academic interests, choose your courses, and fulfill your graduation requirements. These can be very helpful to you in charting your educational experience and exposing you to opportunities that you did not know were possible. They can also keep you on track to make sure you graduate in the appropriate amount of time.

Become a resume editor. This offers several benefits. First, you will meet more of your classmates. Second, you will develop an important skill. And third, you can even earn a little money. If you do not have good resume-writing ability, ask the school's career resources office to teach you, or just visit some of the sites with advice on this topic (e.g. `ResumeDeli.com`). See our chapter on writing resumes later in this book.

Strength

Take leadership as an officer of a student club. Assuming you have a clear idea of the focus of your job search (e.g. the marketing industry), then leadership in the relevant club (logically, the technology, marketing, or advertising club) is an excellent way to build your relationships in that industry and with your classmates.

Choose the extracurricular activities that allow you to grow your leadership skills as well as the breadth of your network. Mandee: I participated in student government while at both college and graduate school. This was an amazing way to interact with administrators, faculty, and students across the campuses. Particularly, by planning social activities, I met a large number of diverse students and connected with them on an easy, relaxed level. I also like to think I had a positive impact on my school.

Arielle Klepach, graduate of Penn and Columbia Law, observes:

> *In college, I was actively involved in a political organization. Being a student leader in a political group allowed me to interact with people who had vastly different views than my own. Again, many of these people are some that I am still in touch with today who now work in law, policy, and government. More than that, though, being a leader in a political organization forced me to have serious discussions with my peers about my views, our differences, and the future of our country. These discussions helped me strengthen my own views in that I was forced to challenge and analyze them in a way that I would not have normally done. My peers who were also involved in other political groups came from a variety of backgrounds, and I know that I would not have had occasion to meet and interact with them if not for my involvement in the organization. (personal communication)*

Even better, work during the school year. Participate in internships, co-op programs, special research projects, etc. This gives you a chance to get to know people further along in their careers who come from a wide range of backgrounds. The best way to build Strength with people is for them to see you in action, and vice versa. Later in this book, we have a section specifically on resources to help you find amazing internships.

Develop mentors. You will *not* have a lot of success in building a relationship with a mentor by saying, "Would you like to mentor me?" Instead, try to get an internship or do something else that's helpful to a mentor. Life is a two-way street: if you can help out someone senior to you, even if it's only doing their filing, you're much more likely to see them be helpful to you.

Join a sports team, no matter how unathletic you are. Serving on the same team is a powerful bonding experience and excellent training for the teamwork skills that are absolutely critical to making things happen in the real world. It will also keep you healthier and more productive. So you're not an athlete? No problem, join the intramural team that has the lowest bar to entry. Maybe your school has a bowling or curling team? Every school has some sports teams that attract those with less sports background. They still have a lot of value in helping you learn how to be athletic. There's a reason that accomplishment in sports is a requirement to win a Rhodes Scholarship (discussed later).

Show up. In person if possible. Lindsey Pollak, Yale graduate and *New York Times* best-selling author of *Becoming the Boss: New Rules for the Next Generation of Leaders* and *Getting from College to Career*, observes:

> *My biggest regret—and, therefore, my biggest recommendation to current students—is to take advantage of the many brilliant professors and visiting speakers on campus. If I had the opportunity to go to college again, I would take classes taught by the very best professors, no matter the subject matter, and attend lectures by as many guest speakers as you can. It is much harder in the "real world" to learn in person from experts and ask them questions directly. Some of my most memorable and valuable experiences include the few classes I took with extraordinary professors and the time I saw one of my idols, Anna Quindlen, speak in person. You can read books and watch online TED talks for the rest of your life; college is the time to learn from as many experts as possible. I'm envious! (personal communication)*

Similarly, Frank Bruni collected surveys from about 30 recipients of the Mitchell Scholarship. He "asked them to reflect on college and to rank, in order of importance, such activities and dynamics as coursework, travel abroad, internships, relationships with classmates, involvement in campus groups, and reading done apart from any class obligation. Relationships with faculty members was also an option, and it was the clear winner, placed near the top by almost all of the scholars and at the top by many."[7] Meet them at office hours; have lunch with them. They're humans too, and by definition they know a lot more about your area of interest than you do.

David Alworth, a research associate in the Center for Business and Government at the Harvard Kennedy School, said,

> *Professors hold office hours for a reason: they want to get to know their students. We hope that you will take advantage*

> *of this time not only to discuss course content but also to develop a relationship. We love to hear about your extra-curricular activities and professional ambitions—and very often, we learn a lot from speaking with you. During office hours this year, I was lucky enough to receive mini tutorials on acapella, competitive swimming, and improv comedy from students who are passionate about these topics and pursuing them outside of class. And whenever I can, I try to incorporate my students' extracurricular passions into class discussions: it's a terrific feedback loop. (personal communication)*

Aaron Buxbaum, a senior tech executive and graduate of Georgia Institute of Technology, observes:

> *By far the best thing I did was get to know my academic advisor/professor better. His courses weren't quite what I was interested going into long term, but I ended up doing three courses with him, including an independent research study, and those experiences collectively gave me an idea of what it's like to actually work in the industry. Pure academia is difficult mentally because you're surrounded and taught by industry experts; meanwhile you're learning basic computer science syntax, and it feels like an impossible climb up to reach their point. Through my experiences with my professor, I learned how large-scale problems are properly solved: by lots of talented people working together, not by one super-talented person alone. (personal communication)*

Repeat back to your conversation partner, in question form, what he or she is saying. This "active listening" will let the other person know you are listening to them. Ask your conversation partner, "If I understand what you're saying, you think that . . ." What's the point of having a conversation unless you reasonably have learned to understand the other person's view?

Use the technology for communicating with professionals which they view as appropriate. Unless a professor explicitly tells you to communicate via social media, we recommend you use phone and email instead of texting, WhatsApp, WeChat, Twitter, or other social media tools. It feels inappropriately intimate and invasive to many professors to receive a text from a student, right next to a text from their spouse. That said, different geographies can have very different cultural norms for which technology platform is considered appropriate. You can't go wrong by asking a professor you meet, "What is the best way to follow up with you? Is email OK?" Email is the universal basic standard for working professionals in the Western economies, so that should be your default assumption.

Use proper phone etiquette. When you call someone, leave a message that includes your name and phone number. Do not expect someone to call you back based on a "hang up," unless you have clarified this previously.

Send texts and emails using proper English and etiquette. Although you probably already finished high school, don't be afraid to refer to textbooks and websites for proper use of English. Plenty of people forget grammar rules, even though the person reading your correspondence may not have. A service like `Grammarly.com` will help you look far more professional.

If texts are allowed, send messages during business hours, between 9 a.m. and 6 p.m., for professional communication, and between 9 a.m. and 9 p.m. for social communication. Nothing damages a relationship like a midnight text. Sending messages at off-hours says, "This was convenient for me, so I decided to run the risk that you would be woken up."

Number

Join as many organizations as are relevant. Typically, each membership costs very little money or is free. As a member, you will be in the loop whenever the clubs have events relevant to your interests. And you will have older peers of whom to ask questions and advice. The lists of alumni can also be quite useful. These clubs also provide multiple points of common connection with your classmates.

Nicole Granet, graduate of the Wharton School of the University of Pennsylvania and current Harvard Business School student, observes:

> *I found mentorship relationships through clubs like Wharton Women, an invaluable source of advice and support. In addition, I relished informal mentorships from older peers I knew through TAing classes, Greek life, and even research*

labs. These remain some of my most prized friendships to this day. (personal communication)

Do something memorable. Chris Yeh, Silicon Valley investor and author, said about his Harvard Business School experience,

In a class of 880 people, it's hard to stand out. But standing out when you're in school delivers disproportionate returns. For example, I was elected one of the three co-presidents of the High Tech and New Media Club. The position came with some fun perks, but it doesn't have much long-term impact once you graduate (when's the last time an employer asked about your student club activities) . . . with one key exception. All the members of my class will always remember Chris Yeh as "the tech guy" or "the start-up guy" for the rest of their careers. It's impossible to develop a personal relationship with all 879 classmates, but you can develop a reputation that allows you to reach all of them.[8]

Build optionality. In the book *The Start-up of You: Adapt to the Future, Invest in Yourself, and Transform Your Career*, Reid Hoffman and Ben Casnocha emphasize the unpredictability of your career. You can help offset that by building relationships with a wide array of people. Whatever your future holds, influential people will likely be able to help you in one way or another.

Diversity

Take diverse classes and build a multidimensional skill set. Don't be afraid to apply lessons from history to assignments in economics. All of the world's most complex problems require solutions that span multiple subject areas. If you take exclusively classes in, say, English and history, you'll only bring a hammer and a nail to the construction site of your life. You need a lot more tools to build something you'll be proud of.

Samantha Kaplan, Goldman Sachs employee and Emory University graduate says:

If I could do college over again, I would do a better job of taking advantage of the diverse course offerings available. You

> *can get wrapped up in your major, and forget that you are in the middle of a campus with so many renowned professors and guest lecturers in many different subject matters. Even in the world of finance, I often draw from disciplines as diverse as history, psychology, political science, and of course, writing. The most successful finance professionals are those who have both quantitative and qualitative skills. Just knowing how to run the numbers is not as effective as knowing what they mean, and how to communicate them to others. (personal communication)*

Start broad and end "spikey." In your academic studies, we recommend sampling a broad range of disciplines before choosing a major. Similarly, when you're picking extracurriculars, we recommend joining a lot of clubs but picking one or two activities to focus on. Many admissions committees confess they prefer applicants who have shown deep commitment and focus on one area, that is, they're "spikey." Similarly, companies deciding who to hire will sometimes ask, "What's your superpower?" Don't join 10 clubs trying to pad your resume; people correctly interpret that as the mark of a dilettante. Pick one or two and become a club officer and expert.

In addition, don't join clubs solely with the goal of helping your long-term career. If you're passionate about juggling, join the juggling club. You'll make friends and get more fit, and that has a lot of value. There's more to life than building out your resume.

Don't forget about your friends from high school and summer camp! Just because you might have moved away from home, there's no need to leave your high school past behind. It is very hard to replace friends you have known since birth, and there is no reason to. Social media makes keeping in touch quite easy.

Jennifer Stein Simms, University of Pennsylvania graduate and an instructor of marketing strategy via UCLA Extension, observes:

> *You never know when you may want to call someone up and ask her something. It always feels awkward when you just want to ask for something without having "maintained" the relationship—send Christmas cards to former colleagues, call on friends' birthdays. Try to keep your network "alive" as you never know when you will need to use it. (personal communication)*

Spend time with diverse people. Don't just sit at the homogeneous table in the dining hall; sit with people who don't look like you. If you're not of Latin American/Latinx origin, for example, but you're spending time with some of the Latin American/Latinx students, you'll have access to a perspective that many of your peers lack.

Read up on all your career options. Use broad career resources like `Glassdoor.com`, `JoinHandshake.com`, and `Vault.com`.

Maximize your number of internships. Take advantage of the fall before you start school, and winter break, as well as the summers, to do internships. There's no harm in asking a firm if you can do a mini-internship or even a DIY internship. Small firms are usually more flexible and receptive to doing internships at nonstandard time slots than large firms with fixed recruiting protocols. We discuss internships later in this book.

Get involved in the entire institution, not just your school or division. For example, many universities let third- and fourth-year students take classes at their graduate departments. Certain clubs, for example, the religious student groups, attract members from across all years and schools within the university.

Do what you love. Deborah Small, a tenured Wharton Professor, observes:

> *At my institution, finance is a very popular major and career path. It is viewed by students as the "high-status" career path. Many students tell me that they feel the pull to "follow the herd" and pursue finance even when they dislike it. This is such a huge mistake! I try to encourage them to include their own well-being in their definition of success and to worry less about how they are perceived by others (easier said than done!). (personal communication)*

5 How to Get the Most Out of Virtual Classes and Events

Once a novelty, virtual learning is now a popular alternative to traditional, in-person education, particularly in communities concerned with minimizing pandemic spread.

For virtual classes, the equivalent to sitting in the front row is to show up very early, participate, and stay late, when only the professor is there. Also, angle the camera so that your face shows up clearly, and the professor can see your facial expressions and maintain eye contact.

Turn off distractions. The temptation to react to electronic notifications while you're home is even stronger than when you're in a room with other people. Eliminate those distractions:

- **Set "Do Not Disturb" or "Focus Assist" on your computer.** Push notifications (the ones that pop into the screen) are the worst distraction.
- **Limit phone notifications.** Ideally, disable your phone and put it out of sight. If necessary, allow exceptions to the "Do Not Disturb" setting on your devices so you can still get a call in case of an emergency.

Mute yourself except when you're speaking. This is considerate to all the other people in the class. However, in a discussion-based course, leave your mic on. You'll annoy everyone if they have to wait for you to turn your mic off mute.

Consider headphones. If your apartment or dorm has a lot of noise or activity, consider a sturdy pair of headphones to block out the noise and keep you focused.

Do not keep multiple tabs open at once in your browser. If you are on a webinar for a class, stick to that screen alone. You might think that other people can't tell when you are reading other pages, but it usually is quite noticeable. Also, the formal research on multitasking shows that, well, it's impossible: you think you can read celebrity news and also process a lecture, but you're inevitably sacrificing your comprehension and recall. Consider using a productivity tool like inmotion.app,[9] which monitors your online activity to help you stay focused.

Set up a formal, dedicated workspace. Knowing exactly where you keep important dates, files, notes, forms, books, and assignments will help you stay on track. Make sure you have a stable Internet connection and the required materials and software for the course. By completing work repeatedly in the same spot, you will establish a routine. Don't do your homework or attend classes on your bed. This hurts your sleep because you associate your bed with studying. You also don't study efficiently, because when you're trying to study, part of your brain associates the location with sleep.

Make sure your backdrop is plain and not distracting, for example, no animals or people walking by. One study found that 44% of respondents prefer to see a wall with books or bookshelves behind the speaker on a videoconference, and 34% prefer framed décor such as art, diplomas, or photographs. Virtual scenic backgrounds averaged only 7% of the vote; we think they're distracting and reduce perceived trust.[10] To help spark conversation, we suggest putting something in the background of your virtual workspace showing your interests. You might put a photo of a landmark from your native country, or your favorite books, or a poster from your sports team.

Invest in good-quality lighting, microphone, and a camera that is at your eye level. If possible, sit facing a window or another light source. Also, avoid sitting with your back to a window. No one wants to stare at a large shadow or a person washed out with light. And no one wants to look up your nostril hair. For advice on your home office technology, we recommend https://www.nytimes.com/wirecutter/office/.

Preempt technical issues. Computers can shut down during a virtual meeting, and most everyone has experienced a spotty wifi connection. First, contact your technical support department if you have one. If the technical problems affect your grades, take screenshots of the issue, communicate with professors, and inform them. IT support teams also often provide training in commonly used programs. Ideally, invest in mobile hotspot capabilities for your phone. That way, if your home wifi is unstable, you have a backup Internet connection.

Use hand movements, within reason. On a videoconference, everyone looks the same: a bunch of quarter-torsos and smiling faces. If you use your hands to talk, people will pay more attention to you, because you'll look distinctive. You'll also be able to emphasize ideas to those who might be unable to clearly see your facial expressions.

Master time management. Even more so than in a traditional classroom, you need to have the discipline to sit down, set goals, and work on assignments until they're done. Online classes offer more flexibility for completing work, but work can't be put off indefinitely. Without solid time management skills, you may easily find yourself cramming before classes or handing in subpar assignments. Everyone benefits from keeping a calendar with assignment due dates and checking it daily; creating a work schedule with designated times for coursework; and reflecting on how you are using your time and making necessary adjustments.

Stay motivated. Keep in mind that online courses are "real" courses just like a traditional, face-to-face, in-person class. You must show up and participate. Set goals at the beginning of the term and at the beginning of each week. Make a list of what you need to accomplish and check off all completed items at the end of the day; this can be a great motivator. If you are having trouble maintaining academic momentum, pair up with a classmate to act as an accountability partner. The more sophisticated online learning platforms will help you to do this, for example, helping you get into a virtual study group.

Clarify expectations. It may be unclear what the teachers' expectations are in an online class. You will need to be even more proactive in asking your professors anything from course expectations to requirements.

Wear "outdoor" clothing, not pajamas. Even if no one sees that you're wearing boxer shorts below the waist, you know you are. A number of academic studies show that what you are wearing affects the quality of your work output.

Wear clothing suitable for video. Shirts with stripes or intricate patterns are distracting. Red, white, and black are also poor choices; we suggest pastel or other light colors. Don't wear noisy or big jewelry, which can be distracting and also make noise. Similarly, shiny eyeglass frames, dangling earrings, or unusual makeup are distractions. We also don't recommend showing cleavage. In person, people can see your whole self; your cleavage is just one facet of you. On a video, your cleavage can become the most visible element people zoom in on.

Get up and stretch. Be sure to get up and stretch between online sessions. Online learning makes it too easy to simply sit at your desk for hours on end. But this lack of movement can result in back and neck problems. A few jumping jacks can really make a difference in your energy level. We suggest a standing desk. For other ideas on how to make your work environment promote fitness, see `https://teten.com/gym`. For ideas on how to make your home environment promote fitness, see `https://teten.com/home`.

Actively participate. Engage in the course's online forum or discussion board. This might involve commenting on a classmate's paper or posting a question about an ongoing project. By checking in often and reading what others are posting, you can get a better understanding of course material and engage with classmates. Even if you have only 30 minutes to spare, a discussion response can be squeezed in. Set a goal to check in on the class discussion threads every day. Don't wait until an assignment is almost due to ask questions or report problems. Knowing classmates can be extremely helpful when preparing for exams, seeking feedback on assignments, or staying motivated. When you're participating in a virtual class or conference, it's very easy to forget about the other attendees and focus all of your energy on engaging with the teacher. But there's no reason you can't meet the other participants in the same way, that you would in the hallways of a traditional event.

Consider putting together a virtual study group. This is a great way to build community when you don't have the advantage of cohabitating.

Direct message classmates and speakers. One huge advantage of a virtual event: you can review the online bios of all the faculty and guest speakers and send direct messages to those that look interesting. You can also message students who, based on their questions, look like folks with whom you have something in common. You should be one of those people who does this. For example, if you're in a class with Sara and see on Instagram that she played water polo in South Florida, you can message her and say, "I see you play water polo; I do too. Did I see you at the Junior Olympics last year?" Or, if you have your sights set on a certain company after graduation, and noticed on LinkedIn that Rebecca worked there last summer, you can message Rebecca and say, "I was reading up on the backgrounds of who's in this class and see that you interned at Microsoft. Could we speak offline about your experience there?"

Make sure other classmates and attendees have your contact information. On some technology platforms, there may be no easy way for attendees to message one another after the class/session ends. No problem. In the group chat, share your direct email with people with whom you developed a relationship. If you say, "I'm looking for a summer internship; email me at ______ if you have ideas," almost no one will write you and you'll just look desperate. Instead, share a "give" not an "ask": "I made a list of all the firms in our city who are actively hiring for graduates with majors in [the subject of this class]. Email me if you'd like a copy." You can also suggest that those who are interested in maintaining contact provide their name and email address in the chat. Of course, be the first to add your own to get the ball rolling. Adding attendees to social media as quickly as possible also ensures that the person knows who you are at the time of the addition and that you don't lose contact after the class is over.

Plant seeds. One of the great challenges of learning virtually is that you don't have random interactions with classmates that allow you to engage in small talk and discover common interests. However, common interests make it much easier for strangers to approach you, and vice versa.[11] In addition to setting up a searchable online profile, a good way to plant seeds is to take social leadership. Consider organizing and attending virtual "Happy Hours" or "Virtual coffees" to provide outlets for new friendships and relationships. Odds are, the other students in your class are eager for direct person-to-person connection as well.

Go where your peers are online. Never had an Instagram or Snapchat account before, but know that several of your classmates use these apps to share and communicate? Are you hearing a lot of jokes in class from TikTok or YouTube? Don't be afraid to meet the other students where they already are.

Have fun! Try getting on calls a few minutes earlier and staying on a few minutes later in order to chat with the other students. Knowing your peers on a personal level always makes a class more fun and interesting.

If You're Not at the Table, You're Missing Out: Plan Your Career

We've both had ups and downs in our career. Here we'll share some lessons. We welcome you to learn from our mistakes.

Think of your long-term goal (manufacturing CEO, real estate developer, judge, impactful journalist, etc.), and then identify the most common path that other people in that job have taken to achieve it. We recommend reading biographies to understand life paths. Even easier: Paulina Symala, a McGill senior starting at Oliver Wyman after graduation, said, "I suggest 'following' people on LinkedIn who are where you want to be 5–10 years from now, and copying what they did to get there. I personally did this to figure out what jobs I needed to take in order to get into consulting" (personal communication). Most very successful people identify a career in which they are interested and for which they are well suited and then work very hard to advance up the relevant ladder for that career. The only real shortcut to success is pure luck, and you can't rely on pure luck to advance your career. To structure your thinking, there are basically three categories of jobs: working in companies or organizations, advising companies or organizations, and investing in companies or organizations. Choose one, and excel.

Consider noncareer goals as well. In addition to work, what else do you hope to achieve in life? Would you like to have children, to live an active outdoor lifestyle, to live close to your family, to perform in a choir regularly? Some careers are better suited for outside interests, and some generate more liquid cash earlier. Hard work in the early years of your career will have a very disproportionate impact on your long-term opportunities. For many students, in the medium to long term they are seeking work–life balance. However, a few years early in your career in a high-stress job working long hours can make the rest of your career dramatically easier. Many employers may assess you in large part based on your early career choices. For example, among the classical fast-track jobs for people interested in business are management consulting and investment banking. If you pursue those tracks early, you are building valuable skills when you are youngest and learn the most. You can milk those early credentials for the rest of your career.

Get to know your school's career office. Don't wait until the last month before graduation to talk with the professionals there, and don't only use it when you start looking for a job. Instead, become familiar with what your school offers, and take advantage of what you may find. Many schools offer help with internships, resume writing, career exploration, mentorships, career fairs, and on-campus recruiting. Many of these program are open to students who are not in their final year. You can benefit by being one of the more forward-thinking students in your cohort.

Do your homework on careers. When you start your education, it's not reasonable for you to know exactly what you want to do after graduation. But it is your job to seek the resources to make an educated decision. Treat your career choice as your most important job. You can't reach a goal that you don't set for yourself!

Attend career fairs. Attending career fairs will allow you to meet industry professionals in a no-risk setting. Ask questions, pick up brochures, and put your name on mailing lists. Don't be afraid to go to the less-populated booths, where you can actually ask detailed questions and have less competition. Remember that you may want to work for one of these companies one day, so be sure to be on your best behavior. That said, there is no way to learn without asking good questions. You're much better off asking your baseline questions with the recruiting representative who went to your school than waiting until your actual job interview.

Join your school's alumni group and attend activities (virtual or not) during breaks from school. Believe it or not, most alumni groups welcome participation from students. There are few things that alumni enjoy more than talking about their college days and hearing about the changes taking place at their college or graduate school.

Mandee: I have been on the board of the Penn Gold Coast Alumni Association for close to 20 years. We love when students come to our events, and always welcome communication from students and new graduates. As an organization, we will actively support the job search of students who want to move to our area. We have an interest in seeing our local alumni base grow and feel a connection to the students from our school.

Create a professional resume and cover letter and share with your career office and trusted advisors for frank feedback. You will need professional resumes and cover letters for internships, fellowships, and even sometimes club membership. Learn how to do it right, and do it well. We will review how to write a resume in a later chapter. Maintain different versions of your resumes for different job roles/functions that you're interested in. For example, a Consulting resume should reflect your business analysis, strategic thinking skills, whereas your Product Management resume should highlight your work around ideating, launching, and scaling new projects. Also, do not hesitate to exclude work experience irrelevant to a role, even if you feel personally attached to it.

Practice interviews. Most educational institutions offer interview preparation through their career office. Prior to an interview, make an appointment to meet with someone to review what you need to know. How you look someone in the eye, conduct a video interview, respond to difficult questions . . . these can make all the difference in getting a job. This is especially important for those who are considering careers in management consulting because the interview questions often include case interview questions, which are unlike those found in other professional interviews.

Learn about professional business etiquette. Mandee: When I was an undergraduate, I took courses in wine tasting and also proper dining etiquette. I did this because they looked like fun, and well, there was free wine. Much to my surprise, my job interview with Goldman Sachs included two dinners at fine dining restaurants. Although I don't recommend that you drink alcohol during an interview, I was thankful for what I had learned about proper formal etiquette.

One student was given the opportunity to shadow a highly renowned physician in the hospital. The young man showed up in jeans and proceeded to call his new mentor by his first name. This not only indicated a lack of professionalism, but also a lack of respect. The physician was so turned off from the initial interaction that the physician never found time for the boy again.

If you plan to attend graduate school, seek planning advice from your college beginning in your first year (or as soon as you decide you're interested). Most colleges have graduate school advisors, particularly relating to pre-med (and various health professions), pre-law, and pre-engineering. You will first want to understand when these advisors start meeting with students and make sure to work toward their timeline. You will need these advisors for letters of recommendation, course selection, and general guidance.

Spend money like a frugal millionaire. Be confident in yourself. If you've been admitted to a reputable school, you can be reasonably certain that you will have a roof over your head after graduation. For example, invest in a nice suit that makes a good impression. We do not encourage spending big dollars on a fancy apartment and high-end lifestyle, disproportionate to your peers. You probably don't want to have a reputation for spending lots of your parents' money. Your parents probably don't want you to develop that reputation either!

Stay open. Although it's valuable to stay focused on your specific long-term career interests, we think school is also one of the rare environments where you are exposed and you can afford to learn about many different fields, not directly related to your long-term goals. We recommend that you make a point of at least getting basic information (e.g. going to company presentations) on one or two fields that you think a priori are not for you. Long-term goals frequently change.

Look for a compatible culture. Although it's great to be a trailblazer, for your first job, stay away from corporate cultures that do not value who you are. Does your selected company welcome women, ethinic minorities, LGBTQ+ people, or another minority groups in which you might be a member? Will you be up against cultural norms that will keep you from learning or reaching your desired goals? Remember that it's much easier to challenge culture when you have some experience under your belt. Every first job is hard. Make sure you accept one in an environment that fits your values and personality.

Christopher Wan, former software engineer at Facebook, and current JD/MBA at Stanford, said,

> *Know yourself, and don't let others define for you what is 'good.' Students at top institutions tend to accumulate gold stars on their resume, for no other reason than because they're gold stars, as defined by society. I find it almost inauthentic that an inordinate proportion of students at schools like Harvard and Yale feel the need to out-compete one another to go to McKinsey and Goldman Sachs post-graduation. To be fair, wanting those things is perfectly fine, as long as you are honest with yourself about why you want them. There are abundant fruits in being an independent thinker and really examining your values and your goals. Don't spend time looking around you: Spend more time looking within. Constant comparison and mimetic behavior lead to a 'herd'*

mentality that almost inevitably results at some point in the realization that your life isn't as fulfilling as you thought it would be. (personal communication)

In business, there is almost never one path to success. Are you a woman considering a career in a predominantly male environment? Do you have religious requirements that might limit your work schedule? How does your chosen profession feel about your gender identity? It's easier to do this introspection earlier rather than later.

Evaluate how important it is to you to work directly on the problems that interest you. There are four ways that you can have an impact on the world, and each has different costs and levels of impact:

First Order: Frontline person. Includes entrepreneur, scientist, activist, organizer, politician, doctor, nurse. You do the hard work of building an organization; you touch the problem directly. This path also has some more meaningful risk because you are on the front lines . . . perhaps literally.

Second Order: Investor/donor. Mandatory part of the ecosystem. You can make change happen by finding and funding the right frontline team members to effect change.

Maybe you really care about the environment, but you're a computer science major and Google is offering you a high-paying job. You may have more positive environmental impact by becoming a software developer and contributing generously to major nonprofits than by working directly for an environmental nonprofit.

Third Order: Advisor. Includes consultants, lawyers, and bankers. You consult with the frontline people but usually don't make the day-to-day decisions.

Fourth Order: Thought leader. Educators, media, authors, journalists, conference organizers. You might be a celebrity and reach lots of people, but your actual ability to change behavior is often limited. You can help to frame the discussion and spotlight certain people, but you have limited power to effect change directly, for example, if you give a keynote slot or a front cover story to a great founder doing work you think important, that can help someone in the crowd to fund/support her. So your impact is indirect.

In Your Final Year Before Graduation

Seek out as much information as possible on options post graduation. Attend information sessions, workshops, special programs, and do some outside reading.

Be opportunistic. Perhaps your long-term goal was to be chief executive officer (CEO) of a start-up company. But you suddenly get an offer to work with a global bank. It's very worthwhile to think about taking it; the relationships and the skills you will develop will have long-term relevance. And you may enjoy working with the firm so much that you reconsider your long-term goal.

Consider the work–life balance you hope to lead, but don't let it define your early career years. Most high potential jobs for young grads require long hours and hard work. Don't be afraid to put in the time you need to learn new skills and build your resume.

Sheryl Sandberg, chief operating officer of Facebook, speaks in her book *Lean In* about how many of her female friends decided to choose jobs with relatively limited work hours, even before they had children or families to balance. Don't assume you can't do it all, or that one spouse (usually the woman) will be responsible for all responsibilities relating to the home. Before you get married, we definitely recommend having a frank conversation with your partner about each of your expected work lives, plans for children if any, and how you expect to allocate responsibilities for running your home together. For more on thoughtfully choosing a spouse, see `https://teten.com/marriage`.

Consider professional help for graduate school. If you are considering graduate school, consult a graduate school advisor.

Mandee: It took me 10 years before International College Counselors started doing graduate school advising, because the knowledge base is so specific. Having someone on your side who knows how to best navigate the graduate school process will ensure that you maximize your options and opportunities. When evaluating graduate school advisors, be sure the professional has experience in your particular area of graduate program. Someone who knows how to apply to law school is not a good fit to advise on a computer science PhD. Be sure to ask the company how many students they have helped in your target area.

Follow a best-of-breed strategy. For example: If you work with a reputable marketing company, then not only can you stay in the marketing industry, but you can also transition relatively easily into other quite different fields. The power of the brand name will dramatically increase the value of your time there. By contrast, if you work at a small regional public relations firm, you are likely much more restricted in your future growth options; you are more restricted to staying in the public relations world, and the lower-tier firms within that world. The marque of your employer is so important that, for example, you should consider working at a reputable consultancy over a third-tier apparel company, even if that industry is your top choice. The reason is that by working at a reputable consultancy, it will be easier for you later to transition over to a well-respected retail company, or even the marketing department of a major company later in your career. You can focus on retail projects at the consultancy, and use that as a platform.

For your first job, we encourage you to avoid the midsize companies, if possible. As a gross and simplistic generalization, we encourage one of two choices: join an academy company like Google, which has great training and an international brand name; or join a small company with an experienced management team, which will give you more opportunities to have a big impact than you can get at a large company. Most midsize companies offer neither the training, brand name, and mentors of a Google, nor the upside and freedom and control of a start-up. Therefore, they typically have less to offer and we're less likely to recommend them.

"When you graduate from school, you should sow not reap," one of our Harvard Business School professors said. "Focus on jobs that give you training to build your core competencies." In other words, although you might be excited to jump into the workforce into a job you're most passionate about, consider your first job out of school as an opportunity to continue to learn and grow. Your degree is a valuable credential, but training at a reputable employer can be an even more valuable credential.

Prepare your letters of recommendation. Asking for letters of recommendation can seem like a simple task, but in fact, getting a strong letter of recommendation requires both time and thought. Remember a letter of recommendation can be saved for graduate school, scholarships and jobs, so it makes sense to cultivate a few good ones, vs. just getting "easy" ones as needed.

Ask someone who has something meaningful to say about you. Remember, the letter should not just tell your grade in a class or your completion of a project, but rather your contribution. Choose someone who knows you over someone who has a fancy title. The readers care about the content first and foremost.

Customize. In many cases, students must send dozens of letters. One of Mandee's female professor friends said that she immediately deletes emails directed to "Dear Sir." Clearly, those students didn't do their homework.

Ask for the letter with as much time as possible before the deadline. Recommenders need time to craft a well- written letter. This is also a sign of respect, that you appreciate the time they are taking and you understand how much they have going on.

Offer to provide information to use for your letter, including a current resume and clear information about the school/ position and deadline. This saves the writer time and effort and ensures that they include information that you think is important for the position.

Make sure that the first request for a recommendation is not an automatic message from a school/employer. When possible, ask for the recommendation in person or via phone. If this is not possible, a polite email requesting a reference letter is appropriate. Remember to ask. If the person makes any indication that they don't have time, or would rather not do so, better to ask someone else than to get a lukewarm recommendation.

Send a polite e-mail reminder a day or two before deadline to confirm that the letter has been submitted.

Send a Thank You note. Showing appreciation is both classy and wise, especially if you need a future recommendation from the same person.

Top 10 Myths Students Believe

When we were students, we had a somewhat naïve set of beliefs about how the world really worked. Only over years did we learn how wrong we were. We've listed here some of the mistaken beliefs we held.

A reputable degree guarantees a reasonable level of competence

David: Most of my worst employees have had degrees from top universities. I fired those people. In hindsight, the reasons for firing were usually apparent during the job interviews, but I mistakenly overlooked those issues in part because of the candidates' stellar academic qualifications.

The skill set in getting into a selective university and getting good grades overlaps with the skill set of being a good team member . . . but it's far from identical. When you're considering joining a company, or hiring your first subordinate, always do your own due diligence and reference checks.

A reputable college degree guarantees success

Your school will expose you to alumni speakers, case studies, and articles about your prominent alumni. That's sample bias. Every school has its failures and embarrassments, from Ted Kaczynski (accepted at Harvard at age 16, Unabomber, convicted murderer) to Jeffrey Skilling (Harvard MBA, McKinsey & Co. partner, Enron chief executive officer [CEO], convicted felon). Statistically, some of your classmates will end up failing in multiple ways, although (we hope) not committing murder or going to prison. As you think about what risks you are comfortable taking, keep your expectations realistic. You can fail just like anyone else, no matter what your pedigree.

You have failed if you do not achieve financial success

Young people often feel intense pressure to continue to succeed in visible ways, through job titles and hefty bank accounts. Success is what YOU define it as. When you compare yourself with others, you are hindering your own self-expression and personal happiness.

We have seen too many classmates give up and take the traditional path, instead of taking a job they see as socially inferior. There's nothing wrong with choosing meaningful work over financial rewards, serving as an artist, social entrepreneur, teacher, politician, or in some other capacity that some of your classmates may not be targeting. That said, make sure you're comfortable with the fact that 20 years from now, you may feel more stressed about paying your bills than your classmates who worked in high-income "boring" professions.

We suggest read Clayton Christensen's seminal Harvard Business Review article, "How Will You Measure your Life?". He encourages people to ponder three questions: 1) How can I be sure I'll be happy in my career? 2) How can I be sure that my relationships with my spouse and my family become an enduring source of happiness? 3) How can I be sure I'll stay out of jail?

You should get to know as many classmates as possible

There's no question that a lot of the value of an education is the network. However, the network is only as valuable as your reputation in that network, and your ability to access it. If people perceive you primarily as the person who's partying every night, or seeking opportunistic friendships, they might hire you for a sales job. But they're probably not going to see you as the analytic genius or the future CEO. By spreading yourself socially thin, you risk not creating any real friendships with people who will truly support you and vouch for your abilities.

Your friends in school will be with you for a lifetime

Your social circle often shrinks steadily between ages 25 and 40, as many people get married and have kids and have less time for casual acquaintances. We both have children, and our social circle has shrunk a lot to focus on the parents of kids the same ages as our children. When you meet your buddies at your reunion, you'll say, "We should get together more often". . . but it usually doesn't happen.

There's no discrimination within your community

The culture of most educational institutions is to be very tolerant and civil. You'll see Republicans and Democrats, Armenians and Turks, Israelis and Palestinians, living near one another, socializing, and working together. This is beautiful, but it doesn't necessarily match what you'll see in the real world. In the real world, people tend to join tribes and to interact and hire with a bias to their tribe. It's human nature, not a Disney movie.

That said, the academic research on social networks shows that people who can cross cultural lines will reap disproportionate rewards. In the discipline of social network analysis, these are known as "structural holes."[12] During your education, you will have a unique opportunity to forge relationships with people quite unlike you. If you can retain those relationships over time, they're a unique asset.

David: For example, I know an American entrepreneur who sources primarily from Chinese manufacturers, leveraging his relationships with some Chinese nationals who went to school with him.

Of course, the fact that people tend to cluster by gender, religion, or ethnicity can also be an advantage. Clubs that organize by student background can be wonderful ways to connect with others of similar backgrounds.

You are so talented that you don't need community

You might think, "I will choose the path less traveled and don't need anyone to achieve my goals." So you follow your passion. You think, "I really care about creativity and self-expression. I will choose a career that allows me maximum creativity and flexibility."

You do that, and perhaps become an artist. Perhaps you're a very talented artist who has done well.

But maybe by staying connected with your classmates, you could have optimized your career through peers who invest in arts, joined museum boards, or simply decorate their homes with beautiful art.

When you run into them at your reunion, you'll realize that by living in a silo, you have missed out on opportunities for growth.

Right after school is a great time to start a company

Mark Zuckerberg (Harvard dropout) and Michael Dell (University of Texas, Austin dropout) get the headlines. However, in reality, most successful entrepreneurs spend quite a few years learning their industries on someone else's dime before they start their businesses. It makes sense to start a company when you have the right balance of clear vision; financial cushion (to withstand the failure risk); experience (to make good decisions); industry knowledge (to give you an advantage vs. competition); and drive. Some people reach that point earlier than others. But wherever you are in life, you should think really carefully before jumping into founding a company. That decision will open many doors for you . . . and close others.

You should join a start-up, any start-up

The argument start-ups will make is that you should join a start-up because of the learning opportunity, high level of responsibility, and potential upside. There's truth to that argument, but only if that start-up is likely to be successful, and/or the management team is highly credible.

Before you join a start-up, one question you can ask: are they backed by a reputable, selective venture capital firm? In particular, note that some venture capital investors are known for a "spray and pray" approach, so their investment should not be seen as a strong endorsement of a given company.

The more conservative path is work for an "academy company" or take one of the traditional jobs for ambitious young people interested in business. "Academy company" is a term for firms that are known for being both very selective in hiring and then providing a high level of training afterward. Think Procter & Gamble, Google, Goldman Sachs, Time Warner, McKinsey, Deloitte, Morgan Stanley, LVMH, Walt Disney, and numerous others.

Among the reasons to take these traditional paths, in lieu of joining a start-up where you'll have more autonomy and make more impact:

- Build universally recognized skills, for example, presentation skills, finance skills, software development skills
- Gain a universally recognized credential
- Build your professional network
- Incur minimal risk
- Learn an industry language

Part of the secret of Silicon Valley's success is that people understand the training you receive even at a start-up. So if you join a start-up run by an Amazon alum, the assumption is that the company is run with some Amazon DNA, and you'll learn some of Amazon's approach to business. Ideally you want to evolve into the sort of professional who has so much credibility that other people want to work for you, because some of your credibility will rub off on them.

You will feel less pressure now that you have graduated from a reputable educational program

Mandee: I've heard too many students say, "X went to Dartmouth, but now he's just teaching high school." Although this is surely an ignorant thing to say, there are too many graduates who feel the pressure of comments such as this one. In certain cases when money is not a problem, it keeps extremely talented people from doing anything at all! But try to remember that if you are worried about what other people define as success, you will rarely measure up.

Write a Resume That Sells

Selling yourself to an employer or graduate school is like selling a car in a magazine advertisement; you have very little space to tell an exciting story to your reader. How can you make the case that you are a must-see candidate?

While in school, both of us worked part time as resume editors. Here are some of the principles we recommended for our fellow students.

Include a permanent address (e.g. your parents' address). Employers like to have a sense of where you are from. However, note that employers may also discriminate against you based on address, so if your permanent address creates that risk, don't include it.

Use a permanent email address (ideally from your university or a domain name you own), rather than using an Internet service provider (ISP) email address (e.g. yourname@gmail.com). Using an ISP email address locks you into that ISP and makes you difficult to reach should you switch ISPs. Better yet, register your family name (e.g, `teten.com`) at namecheap.com or another registrar and get your own email address. Don't use an AOL.com or yahoo.com email; they are considered signs of someone less tech-savvy, who is using older and less capable technology platforms.

"Show don't tell." Instead of "award-winning student," which is vague, try more specific language: "Winner of Most Valuable Student Award." Ideally, insert links to examples of your work. For example, a website you have built, or your personal GitHub.

Be aware of and preempt the prejudices that readers have against you. For example, if you have a nonquantitative education, readers will often assume that you are not good at quantitative thinking. You will benefit by articulating why your reader should not make that assumption.

Similarly, if you grew up in a nonanglophone country, readers will often assume that your English is not truly fluent. You will benefit by mentioning that you have "native fluency in English," assuming that is the truth. You can prove your fluency by talking about your experience teaching, selling, or doing other things that require a very high level of fluency. Particularly if you're participating in many phone calls and videoconferences, speaking readily comprehensible English is a critical life skill. If you have a significant accent, consider investing in an accent-reduction program.

Quantify your achievements. Use numbers whenever possible. "Managed team of 10 first year students." "Turned around underperforming café: moved rapidly to restructure team, and changed net margins from losing money (-5%) to 10%."

Do not fluff. Do not take the risk of weakening your entire document's credibility by including claims that are not credible. Tell the truth and only the truth. When you make claims like "#1 student in fraternity," make sure that you have hard data to support that claim or you will end your interviews very quickly.

Use boldfacing, underlining, and occasionally a box in order to guide the reader's eye to the most impressive portions of your resume.

With the preceding exception, use simple text formatting in your resume: one font size, minimal table usage, no italics, no shadowing, and no graphics. Resumes are often read on a word processing system different than yours, and fancy formatting makes them hard to read and harder to scan. Do not use the automatic bullets in Word; instead, manually type in hyphens. These are more likely to retain their formatting when viewed by a foreign word processor. Save in PDF format to retain your formatting.

Give your resume a name in the format: "LastName-FirstName-Resume-2021.pdf." When the reader of your resume saves the file, it will therefore be easy for him or her to know later what is in that file. Names like "Resume.doc," or even worse, "Tony's Resume.doc," make your reader's job much more difficult.

A resume should answer questions, not ask them. Be careful not to use acronyms and not to leave the reader unclear on your precise history. When readers say, "I don't understand what you were doing in 2020–21," that is your fault and not theirs.

Emphasize your brand names by bolding them and/or writing them in all capital letters. Well-known universities, employers, etc. all carry weight; list them early in the document.

Skim your resume on a mobile phone to force yourself to pay attention to just the most emphasized sections. The average reader spends just 10 seconds glancing at your resume. Evaluate: given that fact, what are the ideas/words that pop out?

Write a summary, but only if needed. If you have no summary statement, you are positioned by the most recent job on your resume. Ask: is that how you want to be positioned?

David: While I was a resume editor in business school, I developed a four-step process for working with my classmates:

1. **Determine what industries and positions you are interested in.**
   If you do not know where you're going, then you certainly won't get there.
2. **Develop a list of the characteristics that your readers are looking for in their applicants.**
   Ideally, you will appear to be precisely the sort of individual that your reader is seeking.
   For example, if you're applying to business school, Harvard Business School used to say explicitly that it sought the following attributes in its incoming students:[13]
   - "**Values and Qualities:** Ethical Commitment, Commitment to Continuous Personal Improvement, Self-Esteem, and Orientation to Action"
   - "**Skills:** Creative Problem Solving, Rigorous Reasoning, Synthesis, Communication and Negotiation, Teamwork and Collaboration, Entrepreneurship, and Leadership"
   - "**Knowledge:** General Management, Functional Expertise, Global Understanding, and Understanding of Technology"
3. **Write the document to highlight specific accomplishments that provide evidence of the reader's desired characteristics and expertise**. When you are writing about your accomplishments, try to write them in the "PAR" structure:
   - **Problem:** What was the challenge?
   - **Action:** How did you overcome it?
   - **Resolution:** What were the specific results of your action?

Here we've given you an example of steps 2 and 3: a list of some common characteristics that recruiters look for, along with suggestions on how to demonstrate that you possess those characteristics. Although these characteristics are common, they may not apply to your particular situation. We have included anonymized text from real resumes of candidates with whom we have worked.

To demonstrate this attribute . . .	here are some suggestions to "show don't tell."
Interpersonal/teamwork skills	"Captain, Ping Pong Team." "Volunteered weekly serving food at homeless shelter." "Member, 10-person team which organized annual fundraising charity ball."
Sales skills	"Raised $100,000 for sorority." "Recruited 20 students to join campus investment club."
Ambition/commitment to continuous personal improvement	"Progressed from yellow belt to black belt in karate in 4 years." "Self-studied Mandarin Chinese and entered program studying at 2nd year level."
Networking skills	"Organized social activities for sorority." "Recruited 5 senior executive speakers to campus; organized public event plus private dinner with them and select student leaders."
Communication skills	"Member, debate team." "Introduced singing group events to audiences in 5 states." "Tutored first-year students in economics."

Personality, humanity	"Train in parkour and bodyweight exercises." "Have traveled to 5 continents, planning trip to #6." Something on the resume to make you more human and approachable, not someone who is focused 100% on business.
Comfort with technology	"Experienced user of Google Office Suite and Microsoft Word, Excel, and PowerPoint." (Don't put this on the resume if you have held a job where it's obvious that you must have mastered these skills, e.g. consultant for a reputable consultancy.)
Comfort with unstructured environment/adaptability	"Traveled independently at age 18 to three countries." "Lived in rural Costa Rica with local family for summer."

The preceding was a list of characteristics. In addition, employers are looking for specific areas of expertise that you have mastered. We've included here a list of topics that you should have some exposure to if you want to work in business, based on the 2020 Harvard Business School first-year curriculum, which subsumes almost all of the major areas of business management. For each of these subjects, list your professional experience that shows you have mastered this topic. If you don't have experience, then you could list the most relevant and impressive courses you took.

To demonstrate this expertise . . .	here are some suggestions to "show don't tell."
Finance, and Financial Reporting and Control	"President, Student Investment Club. Led team to 11.2% annualized IRR (Internal Rate of Return)." "Boosted profit margins from 10% to 14% in student-run coffee shop." "With no PR budget, gained highly favorable press coverage for annual fundraiser." "Negotiated contracts with four customers, increasing revenues 15%."

Leadership and Organizational Behavior	"President, Campus Circus Arts Club, with 30 members and monthly events." "Mentored 5 freshmen who became the next generation of club leaders after I graduated."
Marketing	Managed fraternity's social media account (Instagram, Twitter, TikTok) using Hootsuite.
Technology and Operations Management	Show you think in terms of process improvement: "Reengineered workflow at campus coffee shop to speed preparation of coffee from 15 minutes to 5 minutes."
Business, Government, and the International Economy	Proficiency in multiple languages. Any experience you have studying or living abroad. Any citizenships you have other than your primary one. "Participated in Get-Out-the-Vote campaign, personally soliciting over 200 people door-to-door to vote in midterm elections."
Strategy	"Designed T-shirts with logo showing that Yale won the annual Harvard-Yale football game. When we saw Yale had a big lead in the third quarter, we started printing the T-shirts, and we sold out as attendees left the stadium." This shows that you can plan ahead and take judicious risks.
The Entrepreneurial Manager	"Founded new student club to meet other students who share my passion for parkour."
Leadership and Corporate Accountability	"Lay leader in campus Catholic student group." "Served on student honor court." "Turned down the opportunity to include advertising in our magazine from a local bar with a history of serving students who were visibly drunk."

4. **Finally, double-check your format against the format desired by your reader.** For example, make sure that you have included all the desired information, met all length limits, and answered all questions that are likely to be asked.

Prepare a Personal Marketing Plan

You can make your job search far more efficient by writing a personal marketing plan. This is a document to give to your friends and colleagues to guide them in how to help you in your search. It typically contains a condensed version of your resume, along with details on your areas of focus. In order to give context, it is helpful to attach your full resume to the body of the marketing plan document. Note this should only be shared with close friends and advisors; it will probably seem pompous or presumptuous to most others.

Here is a template personal marketing plan. Of course, please modify based on your own background, interests, and goals.

Experience

(Brief biography)

Nancy has an undergraduate degree in English from Tufts and 2 years writing experience at the *New York Times*. She has primarily focused on climate change and the environment.

Location Preferences (in roughly descending order of desirability)

Nancy grew up in Northern California, now lives in New York, and is open to opportunities in either the New York tristate area, Washington, DC, or Los Angeles.

Target Functions/Areas

Targeting magazines and think tanks focusing on the long-term well-being of the planet.

Ideal Organization Parameters

High integrity. "Academy" organization—known as a training ground for leaders. Blue ribbon management team. Both coworkers and clients are of high caliber. Great mentors. Aggressive growth oriented. Global. Sophisticated. Straightforward, direct. Learning organization. Internet enabled.

Target Industries and Organizations (roughly descending order of preference)

Particularly interested in *National Geographic*, *Time*, *Smithsonian Magazine*, the Carnegie Endowment for International Peace, and the Brookings Institution.

Start Your New Job and Don't Get Fired

Congratulations on your fantastic new job! Now, how do you make sure that you keep it?

According to a recent study, 46% of newly hired employees will fail within 18 months, while only 19% will achieve unequivocal success. Of those who fail, only 11% lacked the necessary technical skills. The overwhelming majority (89%) have other difficulties integrating into the workplace. Coachability, emotional IQ, temperament, and motivation are the most common concerns.[14]

You don't want to be one of those people.

Onboarding is the process of systematic socialization through which employers attempt to preempt those very concerns. You can't rely on your employer to do a good job of onboarding, so let's focus on what you can control: onboarding yourself.

The first thing you should do upon accepting an offer is to wrap up your job campaign. Thank your references and supporters. Withdraw any outstanding inquiries and applications as soon as possible—you don't want to waste their time. Take the extra step of sending a note to the companies that were seriously considering you. If you have your resume online, take it down; your new employer might think that you're still looking for jobs.

Now that you've found a new position, it's time to tell your boss and ensure a graceful exit (assuming you were previously working somewhere else). Whatever happened to make you leave, you don't want to burn bridges or turn good references into bad ones. Give your old boss plenty of notice and do not be confrontational. Take responsibility for wrapping up your projects and helping to transition in a replacement. Keep your head down until the very end, at which point you should personally thank everyone and take your leave. Make sure to stay in touch.

Onboarding doesn't have to wait until your first day of work with a new employer. Conduct extensive research ahead of time. Contact HR to work out logistics (parking, appropriate attire, building codes, lunch, network access, etc.). Identify key stakeholders and schedule lunch meetings. Use the opportunity to introduce yourself and learn what you can about both them and the company.

On your first week with a new company, take it slow. New employees are often nervous and overeager to fit in and contribute. You want both of these things, but charging ahead without knowing where you're going is the surest way to lose momentum and stall out. You'll have huge knowledge gaps starting out, and you likely won't even know where those gaps are. If you don't tread carefully, you'll fall right in as you make mistakes or rub people the wrong way without realizing it. All you can do at this stage is to avoid unforced errors. If you have any questions, the first week is a great time to ask them. You have a limited window during which everyone will be happy to help you and basic questions needn't be embarrassing. Take advantage of it.

In general, be neutral and professional. Don't take positions on issues until you understand why different reasonable people have different positions on that issue.

Your next goal should be to map out the environment. First, learn the culture. What does the company value? How do you get things done? What sort of behaviors are rewarded or penalized? What are the norms for interacting with colleagues? Second, study office dynamics. Identify the various cliques and their members. Get a sense of what sort of terms people are on. Understand the agendas underlying outward behavior. This information will be valuable later on. Finally, learn the styles and expectations of key people.

Learn how to read your boss. Next, you should figure out who relies on you and what they need. Also scope out your own dependencies, so you can be sure that you have good relationships with those people.

Once you're off to a good start and understand the environment, you'll need to start navigating office politics. You are a part of office politics whether you like it or not. Even staying completely neutral and aloof can have negative repercussions. Once you're settled, we particularly recommend figuring out ways to take internal informal leadership; you can't take formal leadership until you've been there for a longer time, for example, organize a group activity, like a group fitness class.

Aggressively build your network. In a traditional office, the ability to cultivate relationships around the office cafeteria and water cooler is invaluable. This "whisper network" will tell you about internal job openings early, warn you about bad bosses, and tell you everything else that HR won't tell you.

However, if you're working primarily virtually, you won't be able to rely on these relationships forming organically. As a substitute, we very strongly recommend that you proactively reach out to other interns, graduates of your program who work at the same firm, and anyone else internally and request to have "virtual lunch" with them. The worse they can say is no, and most likely they'll admire your proactive nature.

David: When I was a college junior, I interned at Procter & Gamble, a $300 billion valuation company. The then-chief executive officer (CEO) was John Pepper, a Yale grad. I sent his admin an email requesting to have lunch. In hindsight, I'm amazed that he agreed, and we had a one-hour lunch in his private dining room.

Lastly, we recommend signing up for the mailing lists for the networking groups, trade associations, nonprofits, and so on that interest you. This is by far the fastest and easiest way to make new friends. This is most important if you're moving to a new city.

11 Write a Memo People Actually Read

We both spent many late nights as investment bankers and strategy consultants early in our careers. Our #1 learning from that experience (besides how to pull an all-nighter) was how to communicate in an effective way, particularly with senior executives.

Our thoughts here may remind you of a school paper. The reality is that writing a business memo and writing a paper for school are very similar exercises, so please don't let the academic tone mislead you.

When we first started work, it took us a while to understand why our managers were so obsessive about editing, formatting, and proofreading. After a while, we finally understood: the reason is that your readers use your editing as a proxy for the diligence that goes into your underlying work. If they see a misformatted number, they assume there are significant errors in the underlying analysis. They assume you're competent unless they're given a single reason to assume otherwise . . . and then they assume you're not competent.

Checklist for Writing a Business Memo

Create a thesis. Before writing, identify your thesis, or argument.

Structure. Create an outline, preferably using the outline feature in your word processor.

David: The bullets in the outline should be mutually exclusive and collectively exhaustive ("MECE"), a concept I learned in strategy consulting that is surprisingly broadly applicable.

The introduction should announce the topic and why it matters, provide/link to necessary background material, and define key terms. You should also acknowledge the limitations of your analysis (budget, time, and your biases, for example).

The conclusion should summarize the main points, and indicate the next steps.

Background research. Collect research. Demonstrate your diligence and level of thoroughness by referencing experts and using footnotes. Ideally every claim is backed by data that you sourced, or you link to your source.

Include illustrations/graphics if appropriate. Images are far more impactful than text or numbers.

Style. Pick a formatting style and stick to it; for example, if all titles are bold and headlines are in caps, make sure this is consistent throughout the paper. We suggest using a tool like Grammarly, which identifies grammatical errors, and makes suggestions on style and tone of delivery.

In school, you're taught to write in paragraphs with no formatting. In a professional environment, a very common style is to write in paragraphs with your subject line bolded, summarizing all material information in that paragraph. Much of this book is written in this style. This format is easier for busy readers to skim.

Use clear and concise sentences; avoid jargon and the overuse of unnecessarily polysyllabic verbiage; that is, speak simply.

Less formal documents, such as memos, need not use formal language. However, they have a specific format. They are typically short and are used to clearly and quickly address specific actions or management tasks.

So what? Include the key takeaways of your analysis before every section. Your colleagues may not read through the entire deliverable, so make it easy for them to understand the key points.

Edit. Review for common mistakes (run-on sentences, plural versus possessive, subject/verb agreement, comma usage, etc.).

If this is a critical memo, solicit feedback from a friend or colleague. Some questions to ask:

- What is my argument/thesis/main point? If the reader can't answer that, you have a problem.
- Do you think I successfully support this with evidence?
- Is the evidence convincing?
- What didn't you understand?
- Does each paragraph distinctly and clearly progress the thesis?
- Do paragraphs have appropriate transitions?

Present So People Will Hear

Presenting in front of a group of peers or even a 1,000-person audience is an extremely valuable skill. You might speak, but does the audience hear what you're saying? And do they believe it?

David: When I was in graduate school, someone told me that one of the hardest skills to practice is public speaking. The reason is that it requires an audience. To practice tennis you only need one friend but to practice public speaking you need a room full of people. So in order to build that skill, you should always volunteer for every opportunity to get yourself in front of a crowd. I did that repeatedly, to the point that people started paying me five figures to keynote at finance and tech industry conferences.

In this chapter, we discuss the key principles to making an effective presentation. The first consideration is to decide whether you're writing presentation slides for presentation or for reading. If you are preparing slides for presentation, you should put as little text as possible on each page, so that your readers can focus on you, the presenter, rather than the pixels in front of them. Powerful graphics are critical.

But: if the deck is designed for reading, you can and probably should write in full, detailed sentences. You don't need to be shy about including a significant amount of text.

Lead with a clear and compelling message. The slide deck should tell a story, with a beginning, a middle, and an end.

A slide should answer any questions immediately raised by the slide. For example, if a revenue number looks extremely high but is actually correct, explain what happened in a footnote.

All slide titles should answer the journalist's classic six questions:

1. **Who?** Include the source of the data if applicable. If it's your work gathering data and crunching, you can write something like "Proprietary analysis" or "Original research."
2. **What?** Specify subject and, especially, units of chart. On September 23, 1999, NASA lost the $125 million Mars Climate Orbiter spacecraft after a 286-day journey to Mars. Why? Lockheed Martin, which was running certain critical calculations, was sending thruster data in English units (pounds) to NASA, while NASA's navigation team was expecting metric units (Newtons). Units matter.
3. **Where?** Indicate location of data or study. There's a big difference in meaning and applicability if your data set covers only the United States, as opposed to covering the entire world.
4. **Why?** Show how the slide moves the presentation forward. How does it relate to the presentation's themes? For example, "Net Increase in Population, 1990–2020" is more informative than "Population Trends, 1990–2020."
5. **When?** Indicate for what time periods the chart is appropriate. Double-check if you're analyzing calendar years, fiscal years, or academic years.
6. **How?** If possible, show how data were collected. For example, whether the data show consumption of soft drinks vs. amount of soft drinks entering distribution channels will affect the interpretation of the numbers.

Label your charts clearly. Everyone has his or her own style of formatting chart titles; most important is to be consistent within one presentation deck. Here's a sample six-part structure that can be used for almost any slide headline and title, which collectively addresses the preceding six questions:

Headline	Car sales per capita have dropped significantly due to economic downturns, cultural change, and growth of car-sharing.
What the chart actually measures	US car sales per capita

How the data are being split, for example, by category or by state	by gender
Year(s)	1990–2020
Units in parentheses	(M)
Source (bottom of slide)	National Automotive Dealers Association, nada.org, as of May 1, 2021. Based on reports from individual auto dealers.

Label all chart axes. Tick marks should be outside of the graph, which looks visually cleaner than if they cross the axis.

Consider your audience and venue when structuring your slide style. In general, use the largest font sizes you can: 18 point and up. No one ever complains about fonts being too big. Also, use as few words as possible on each slide, or better yet, use images instead of words. This is particularly important if you're presenting virtually, because people may be looking at your slides on a phone or side by side with your face on a virtual presentation service.

Use fewer slides to leave more time for discussion instead. Guy Kawasaki, Silicon Valley entrepreneur and marketing specialist, recommends a maximum of 10 slides for 20 minutes.

Minimize technical terms, unless you know for sure all of the audience is within your specific industry and will understand all of the terms.

Use slide trackers (which show where you are in a presentation) for longer presentations, for example, a progress marker at the top of the slide that shows how much you have progressed through a given presentation.

David: Here is an example from the top of a presentation I gave on how to use technology to accelerate sales:

The presentation has five parts, and as I walk through it, it highlights in dark blue a different tab on the progress bar. You can see other examples at `https://teten.com/speaker`.

Design your slides to be attractive even at high resolution. Make sure your images are not unclear when projected onto a big screen. The safest bet is to go for the highest resolution that you can find.

Animation between slides can be distracting, so keep animation to a minimum unless necessary. Also, many people print out slides, which makes your animation irrelevant. In most cases animation is extra work for too little payoff.

Always use dark text on light backgrounds or light text on dark backgrounds. Often, using highly contrasting colors can cause eye strain on the audience, so go for light gray on black and vice versa. Be careful of color combinations such as red on green; about 7% of all men are color blind to some extent.

Look for memorable graphics. Graphics speak louder than words. The best type of graphic is data supporting your thesis. If you don't have good data on a given point, then we suggest using a memorable, interesting, and/or funny image. Including attractive images that dramatize your speaking points will significantly increase your efficacy as a speaker.

In picking images for a presentation, we see two main risks. The first is picking an overly obvious image. An image of people holding hands to represent teamwork falls into this category; it is trite and almost insulting. The second risk is using an image that is too creative for the audience to discern the immediate relevance to the topic at hand. William Zinsser observed in his influential book *On Writing Well* that if you're reading your own work and find a gem of a phrase that sticks out of your text, save it for future reference, but delete it from your text as a distraction. Our goal in presenting images is similar; the image should be clearly relevant, but still clever and unique.

So we recommend that you brainstorm different ideas for an appropriate image, and then look for pictures or drawings that reflect our vision of what a good graphic should be. Google Image search is a great place to look for inspiration but a bad place to find images you can use legally. Your legal rights to use images you find randomly on the Internet are a gray area for three reasons:

- The major search engines do not have accurate filters to distinguish between copyrighted and noncopyrighted images.
- It is often difficult to know whether the image you are using is in its original form or copied from another site.
- A page does not have to list copyright information for a picture for that picture to in fact be considered copyrighted.

There are some safe picture selection options, however. You can use `search.creativecommons.org`, which restricts your search to images that are licensed for use under Creative Commons. Just tick the appropriate boxes based on whether you plan to modify the image and/or use it for commercial purposes. Other good options are `https://flickr.com/creativecommons` and `Unsplash.com`.

Consistency, consistency, consistency. Use master (template) slides to standardize slide layouts.

All repeated figures must be internally consistent. For example, frequently a company's annual volume or revenue appears on multiple slides. That number must always be the same. All titles and terms (company names, brand names, etc.) must be spelled and punctuated consistently.

Tidy numbers and all other data. Check for consistency with decimal points and abbreviations used across the deck. Use the standard abbreviations for numbers, for example, K = Thousand, M = Million, B = Billion.

Always differentiate clearly hard numbers from estimates, either in a footnote or with an "est." for each figure that is an estimate.

Always show sources for data in a footnote, and explain any anomalously high or low data point in a footnote.

All percentages should add up to 100. If it does not add up due to a rounding issue, then either footnote "Does not add up to 100 due to rounding" or increase your units of precision used. When a slide title or axis indicates that the units are dollars or percentages, you should not have a dollar sign or a percentage sign after each number. They clutter the slide.

Name your file for version control. We recommend naming each file with the suffix in the format yyyymmdd, in order to track the most current version of a given file. For example, 20210513 is the label for a file last modified as of May 13, 2021.

Use our "CLEAN" checklist to proofread a slide:

> **Consistent**: Assume the reader will look at the document with a calculator in hand, checking that every number ties with every other number. All repeated figures must be internally consistent. Breakdowns of the sources of change should add up to the total change shown; slide segments should tie with the total. All titles and units must have a consistent format across slides. And of course, the formatting must be internally consistent.

> **Language**: All titles and terms (company names, brand names, etc.) must be spelled and punctuated accurately and consistently. Is the language unambiguous?

Elegance: Is the slide elegant, clean, and attractive? Does it follow one single style template?

Auditable: Have you included a sources line for each data point, so the reader can easily audit the accuracy of your work? Have you precisely indicated the time period and geography of all data sets? Have you included the complete file name somewhere in the presentation? Look for unusually low or high numbers; anything that looks at all strange should be double-checked with your original data source, and footnoted if appropriate. It's far better for you to notice your errors/issues than for someone else to do so.

Next Steps: Make it clear what you want the reader to do.

13 Easy Career Kickstarts That Most People Don't Do

Once you start work in an organization, even if just as an intern, you will be held accountable to a much higher standard of professionalism. We've listed here 10 simple kickstarts that will put you well on the way to being a top contributor to any organization.

In general, most people flake. If you're not a flake, you are far more likely be trusted, promoted, and funded.

David: Back when I was an entry-level employee, the trainers gave us some basic advice on how to be a good financial analyst. At the time these sounded obvious, but now with hindsight we think that most of your success in your career is just executing on these basic points . . . whether you're a chief executive officer (CEO) or aspire to be a CEO.

Listen, and write down what you hear. David: The trainers at my first job out of college told us to always carry a notebook, because clients and your colleagues will ask you to do tasks. If you write down those tasks and actually execute them, you become known as someone worth asking to do stuff. When I meet a start-up founder seeking to raise capital, I often will make suggestions of people for them to meet, competitors to analyze, or ideas to pursue. I don't expect them to follow up on any particular suggestion; I'm just one opinion out of many. However, I do note if they are writing down suggestions. If not, that indicates that they may not be the sort of person who's diligent about listening to the market. Not good. Why take that risk?

In general, say yes to every opportunity to demonstrate responsiveness. If a colleague poses a question to which you have no idea of the answer, just say, "Let me research that."

Organize your data. Successful people are careful to retain and organize all of their notes: on meetings, people whom they meet, assignments for which they have responsibility, and so on.

In a meeting, we recommend take notes on paper, using a digital pen, or (typically last choice) with a computer keyboard. Using a computer requires looking at the screen instead of making eye contact. It also often makes people feel that you're not paying full attention to them, but instead checking your messages.

Mandee: I actively use the notes feature on my computer—keeping track of to-do lists and details that I don't want to forget. Also, when there is a meeting that's important, I add an alarm to my phone, ensuring I don't come late or miss the appointment altogether. I also add little notes to contacts in my address book, such as "Met at: climate change conference April 5, 2021. Family: two kids same age as mine." That way, when I am speaking with that person again, I am sure to remember our previous interactions.

Find the instructions and follow them. You have the sum of all the world's knowledge in your pocket. Before you do any task, look for the instructions.

David: For example, I am amazed at how many cover letters clearly indicate that the student didn't do background research before approaching an employer. If a job candidate doesn't do some basic research before approaching employers, that's a bad sign for their ability to operate autonomously.

Don't reinvent the wheel. Lilin Wang, now a software engineer at Google, observed that 80% of technical problems she tries to solve in her projects have already been tackled by others. If you look for solutions on a search engine or forums such as Stack Overflow before you do a task, you typically will save a lot of time. And include your sources: make sure to footnote/link to the origin of any data that you quote/models that you emulate.

Overcommunicate. If you don't understand the goal of a task, or believe it has already been accomplished by someone somewhere but require help in locating it, just ask. On the flip side, if you envision a way to produce a better result/product, communicate that to your colleagues and ensure it is aligned with their intended goal. Either way, you are making sure you are not wasting your time and reinforcing a relationship with your colleagues.

Double-check. The smartest person doesn't necessarily get promoted. Rather, it's the person who catches the inevitable mistakes and fixes them. It's critical to double- and triple-check your work. Whether it's a text for a tweet or a fundraising deck, Raffi Sapire, formerly director of operations, LivePeer, prints out and rereads every piece of content before sending to her team. One of the marks of a good financial modeler is building checksums throughout her model; the analogous principle holds for a good software developer.

Lisa Shalett, formerly a partner at Goldman Sachs, observes that there are two buckets of things: those you can control and those you can't control. For the things you can control, you should nail them.

Follow up. If you ask someone to do something, set up a reminder to make sure they actually executed it.

David: When I meet people, I often say, "Please email me [a business plan/a competitive analysis/a resume/etc.]." Only 20% of people whom I meet actually follow up. Not good.

One way to think about this is to learn to be "professionally pushy." In *Getting Things Done*, David Allen talks about the "Waiting For" list, to keep track of follow-ups you are waiting for from others.

Mandee: I track my outstanding requests on my calendar. I usually ask my students to get back to me on a certain date. Then, on that date in my calendar, I add a note, "Did Penelope get back to me with her college essay? Did Matthew call me as discussed?" My students are always amazed at how they are held accountable for every item requested!

David: I send out a lot of emails asking people to do things. If it's an important request, I'll typically star it in my Sent Messages folder. Every 2 weeks or so I review my starred messages and see if there are any people I need to nudge to get back to me. The people I work with know that I'll follow up, which encourages them to revert sooner rather than later.

Play nice and be nice. Early in your career, you typically advance based on technical skills. But very rapidly, your ability to work cooperatively with people inside and outside the firm is a big driver of your advance.

Think differently. Bring one idea to the table each month that would help your company or team achieve its goals and objectives for the year. Thoroughly think through the steps you will take to execute on that goal and which stakeholders need to be involved at certain points. Even if only two ideas receive positive feedback and a go-ahead, highlighting your ability and history of disrupting the status quo is helpful when promotion discussions come around.

Study your future resume. In every industry, there are certain leadership programs, clubs, activities, and other credentialing paths that smooth your way to success. Look on LinkedIn and in resume databases at people who look like who you want to be, 5 years from now. Copy what they did. Amateurs copy, geniuses steal.

14 What You Will Know by Age 45

The entering students in your cohort are likely relatively homogeneous. They're mostly the same age, generally ambitious. They're also much luckier than most of the country, insofar as students are on average healthier and more likely to come from intact families than people of the same age who are not in full-time education.

However, by our 20th reunion, we found there was far greater dispersion of paths in life. By the 20th reunion, we would estimate about 10% of our peer group were on the tracks that they had hoped to be on that point: Industry leaders, professionals, entrepreneurs, etc. The difference in wealth creation between the top 10% and everyone else was staggering.

Likewise, our classmates had varied stories about personal health and happiness. Some were making very healthy incomes and were industry leaders but in some cases had sacrificed marital stability to achieve that. Others had focused on the family and stopped working full time. Others were now focused on working in the nonprofit sector, as a way they could give back. Financial success is easy to quantify, but money is definitely not the only driver of your overall happiness.

David: here are vignettes from some my classmates. I list these just to show that no matter where you go to school and work, life throws up unexpected hurdles.

- **Six graduate school classmates had passed away by the 20th reunion (out of about 850).**
- **A number of classmates had very material health problems:** cancer, debilitating auto accidents, multiple sclerosis, Guillain–Barré syndrome.
- **Quite a few friends got divorced** . . . massively destabilizing in itself and also typically very negative for career choices and

options. For example, one high-flyer with a golden resume got married, moved, and had three kids. Then he divorced. Now he is effectively locked into living in the region where his ex-wife lives, which is a region with relatively poor fit for his skill set. At `https://teten.com/marriage`, I discuss how to choose a partner thoughtfully.

- **Quite a few people explicitly said they took jobs in part for lifestyle reasons.** They were tired of travel and not seeing their family. One executive had a child with cancer (since recovered) and remarked that he was getting out of his business to do something else and take care of his child. Some more common career paths for people who wanted a flexible lifestyle: recruiters, private bankers, professors, entrepreneurs.
- **A few graduates left the business world entirely**. I know of Harvard Business School alumni who became composers, physicians, screenwriters, artists, firefighters, writers, religious leaders, and singers.

We know that your career will likely have a lot of starts and stops. But the only person who needs to feel satisfied is you.

15 Internships and Other Work Experience, Locally and Globally

David: I used to work for a senior investment banker in his 40s. I noticed on his resume he still listed his McKinsey & Co. MBA summer internship. I suspect he didn't even get a job offer in his senior year, but he still got reputational benefit by being a McKinsey alum.

As a young person, you have the unique opportunity to work for a wide range of companies, in many locations, without anyone wondering why you're hopping around between industries and employers. Take advantage of it! You'll never again be able to eat from a "tasting menu" of job options.

You have nothing to lose by asking. Don't hesitate to approach any company that interests you about an internship, or perhaps asking them to host you for a research project for school. In addition, a number of firms will help find internships, for example, Adout International (adouti.com; specializing in Francophone students), Dream Careers (www.summerinternships.com), Intern Group (theinterngroup.com), and GEOInterns (geointerns.com). These firms typically charge you a fee for doing so.

In addition to the major job boards and your school's specific resources, we suggest these resources:

Chegg Internships

https://www.chegg.com/internships

Exhaustive resources for interns.

Parker Dewey

parkerdewey.com

"Parker Dewey offers the largest network of highly motivated college students and recent graduates who are excited to complete short-term, paid, professional assignments."

Riipen

riipen.com

"Riipen helps students get work experience with real companies for course credit."

We've listed here some programs that specialize in helping you find work experience abroad or help non-Americans find internships in the United States.

Center for International Career Development

CICDGO.com

Eligible: American and international college and graduate students

"Center for International Career Development (CICD) provides university students, graduates, and young professionals with opportunities for practical career training abroad."

Experiential Learning International

eliabroad.org

"A non-profit organization that creates volunteer and internship opportunities for the globally-minded seeking a travel experience that goes beyond the ordinary."

One To World

one-to-world.org

Eligible: American and international college and graduate students

"One To World fosters intercultural understanding by creating face-to-face experiences among local communities, international students, and Fulbright scholars." Particular focus on the New York area.

Tamid Group

tamidgroup.org

"Students may choose to join student-led consulting teams that advise Israeli companies on the solutions to important business problems. Members can also choose to join the Investment Fund program, in which teams conduct equity research and manage a stock portfolio. Each summer, members have the opportunity to spend 8 weeks in Israel on our capstone internship experience."

16 Get Paid to Study: Ridiculously Generous Scholarships

We have listed here some of the most generous, selective, and impactful scholarships. We also list the most interesting learning opportunities for people interested in technology; math, engineering, and science; and social impact. Many of the organizations we list offer contests with cash prizes, workshops, honoraria or stipends, and other career accelerators.

We cannot hope to be fully exhaustive. We encourage you to start scholarship research by searching the major scholarship research sites listed here.

Scholarship Databases

CareerOneStop Scholarship Finder (US Department of Labor)

https://careeronestop.org/toolkit/training/find-scholarships.aspx

"Search more than 8,000 scholarships, fellowships, grants, and other financial aid award opportunities."

College Board

https://apps.collegeboard.com/cbsearch_ss/welcome.jsp

"Find scholarships, other financial aid and internships from more than 2,200 programs, totaling nearly $6 billion."

Fastweb

fastweb.com

"Fastweb is your connection to scholarships, colleges, financial aid and more."

ProFellow

profellow.com

"ProFellow is the go-to source for information on professional and academic fellowships, created by fellows for aspiring fellows."

Student Scholarship Search

studentscholarshipsearch.com

"An organized platform for students to search, investigate and apply for scholarships."

US Department of Education, Office of Postsecondary Education—Information for Students

https://www2.ed.gov/students/prep/college/index.html

For US citizens.

USA Study Abroad

https://studyabroad.state.gov/us-government-scholarships-and-programs/us-college-and-university-students

For study abroad by US citizens.

The Elite Scholarships

Beinecke Scholarship

beineckescholarship.org

Eligible: College juniors

"Each scholar receives $4,000 immediately prior to entering graduate school and an additional $30,000 while attending graduate school. . . . in the selection of a graduated course of study in the arts, humanities and social sciences."

Gates Cambridge Scholarship

gatesscholar.org

Eligible: Undergraduate and graduate students who are not citizens of the United Kingdom

"Each year Gates Cambridge offers c. 80 full-cost scholarships to outstanding applicants from countries outside the UK to pursue a full-time postgraduate degree in any subject available at the University of Cambridge."

George J. Mitchell Scholarship

https://us-irelandalliance.org/scholarships.html

Eligible: Undergraduate students who are US citizens

"Up to twelve Mitchell Scholars between the ages of 18 and 30 are chosen annually for one academic year of postgraduate study in any discipline offered by institutions of higher learning in Ireland."

Harry S. Truman Scholarship

Truman.gov

Eligible: US college juniors

"The scholarship offers . . . up to $30,000 to apply toward graduate study in the U.S. or abroad in a wide variety of fields . . . in preparation for a career in public service."

Luce Scholarship

https://hluce.org/programs/luce-scholars

Eligible: College seniors, graduate students, and young professionals

"The program provides stipends, language training, and individualized professional placement in Asia for 15–18 Luce Scholars each year."

Marshall Scholarship

marshallscholarship.org

Eligible: Undergraduate students who are US citizens

"Marshall Scholarships finance young Americans of high ability to study for a graduate degree in the United Kingdom."

Rhodes Scholarship

RhodesScholar.org

Eligible: Undergraduate students who are US citizens

"The Rhodes Scholarships are the oldest and most celebrated international fellowship awards in the world . . . . provides full financial support . . . to pursue a degree or degrees at the University of Oxford in the United Kingdom."

The Rotary Global Grant Scholarships

https://my.rotary.org/en/document/global-grant-scholarship-supplement

Eligible: All applicants must be a member of a qualified Rotary club

"Global grant scholarships fund graduate-level coursework or research for one to four academic years."

Schwarzman Scholars

schwarzmanscholars.org

"The program gives the world's best and brightest [college graduate] students the opportunity to develop their leadership skills and professional networks through a one-year Master's Degree at Tsinghua University in Beijing."

Siebel Scholars

siebelscholars.com

"Siebel Scholars recognizes the most talented students at the world's leading graduate schools of business, computer science, bioengineering, and energy science. . . . Each receives a $35,000 award toward their final year of graduate studies."

Thomas J. Watson Fellowship

https://watson.foundation/fellowships/tj

Eligible: Graduating college seniors

"The Thomas J. Watson Fellowship is a one-year grant for purposeful, independent exploration outside the United States, awarded to graduating seniors nominated by one of 41 partner colleges."

Udall Foundation Undergraduate Environmental Scholarship

https://udall.gov/OurPrograms/Scholarship/Scholarship.aspx

Eligible: Sophomore and junior level college students committed to careers related to the environment

"The Udall Foundation awards scholarships to college sophomores and juniors for leadership, public service, and commitment to issues related to Native American nations or to the environment."

Technology

We've included in this section the most impactful programs we've found for students and young professionals interested in technology. For a list of free and low-cost educational programs to learn about venture capital specifically, see http://teten.com/vced.

HackNY Fellow

hackny.org

Eligible: Full-time undergraduate and graduate students

"Since 2010, hackNY has empowered a community of student-technologists in New York City through the annual Fellows Program and student hackathons."

InSITE Fellows

insitefellows.org

Eligible: Students who attend graduate school within the United States.

"InSITE Fellows at 7 chapters across the nation engage in semester-long consulting projects for emerging companies, in addition to chapter-specific curriculum and networking events."

Kleiner Perkins Fellows

fellows.kleinerperkins.com

Eligible: Students who attend a college or university within the United States

"Over the course of a summer, KPCB Design and Engineering Fellows join our portfolio companies, where they develop their technical or design skills and are mentored by an executive within the company. Participants in our new Product Fellows program will get the chance to spend a full year working at a Silicon Valley startup."

Thiel Fellowship

thielfellowship.org

Eligible: People under 22

"The Thiel Fellowship is a two-year program for young people who want to build new things. Thiel Fellows skip or stop out of college to receive a $100,000 grant and support from the Thiel Foundation's network of founders, investors, and scientists."

Venture for America

ventureforamerica.org

"VFA is a two-year fellowship program for recent grads who want to work at a startup and create jobs in American cities."

Science, Engineering, and Math

Center for Applied Rationality

rationality.org

Eligible: Flexible

"A nonprofit founded to give people more understanding and control of their own decisions and behavior." Runs regular workshops. The American version of the European Summer Program on Rationality, also listed here.

European Summer Program on Rationality (ESPR)

espr-camp.org

Eligible: "We're looking for participants who are 16–19 years old."

"The curriculum covers a wide range of topics, from game theory, cryptography, and mathematical logic, to AI safety, styles of communication, and cognitive science. The goal of the program is to help students hone rigorous, quantitative skills as they acquire a toolbox of useful concepts and practical techniques applicable in all walks of life. ESPR's tuition, room, and board are free for all admitted students . . . Need-based travel scholarships are also available."

Jet Propulsion Laboratory (JPL)

https://jpl.nasa.gov/edu/intern/apply/visiting-student-research-program

Eligible: College and graduate students

"The JPL Visiting Student Research Program, or JVSRP, offers research opportunities to students who have a compatible research interest with NASA/JPL and have secured funding from third-party sponsors who are not associated with NASA or JPL funding sources."

Mathematical Association of America: Research Experiences for Undergraduates

https://maa.org/students/reustuff/pages/REU.html

"Research Experience for Undergraduates (REUs) are summer programs sponsored by the National Science Foundation (NSF). REUs usually consist of two parts: intensive study of topics through lecture and interaction, and student research on a question/questions. Travel costs are paid for as well as room and board. A stipend is given to participants."

Santa Fe Institute Complex Systems Summer School

https://santafe.edu/engage/learn/schools/sfi-complex-systems-summer-school

Eligible: Graduate students

"The Complex Systems Summer School offers an intensive 4-week introduction to complex behavior in mathematical, physical, living, and social systems."

Social Impact

You can see a list of all the foundations and other institutions that provide financial support for technology-enabled social impact initiatives at `teten.com/impactsupport`. Some specific programs focused on students follow.

Millennium Campus Network

`mcnpartners.org`

Eligible: College and graduate students interested in making a social difference in the world

"The Millennium Campus Network (MCN) is a Boston-based, global non-profit training the next generation of social impact leaders. Through an innovative year-long experience, the MCN is training a new generation of leaders on university campuses across the globe."

World Summit Awards for Young Innovators

`https://worldsummitawards.org/wsa_categories/youth-innovation-category`

Eligible: Young social entrepreneurs under 30

"The WSA Young Innovators is a special recognition for young social entrepreneurs under 26 years of age, using ICTs [information and communication technology] to take action on the United Nations Sustainable Development Goals (UN SDGs)."

High School Only

Rise `https://www.risefortheworld.org/`

Eligible: Anyone in the world ages 15–17

"Each year, 100 Rise Global Winners will receive a lifetime of individualized support...Rise benefits could exceed USD 500,000 for every Global Winner over the course of their lifetime, depending on need, making this one of the largest scholarship programs—if not *the largest*—in the world." Rise is a partnership between the Rhodes Trust and Schmidt Futures.

17 Politics and International Relations

Leon Trotsky apocryphally said, "You may not be interested in war, but war is interested in you." Even if you're not interested in politics, you live in a political system and you will benefit by understanding it. In this chapter, we've listed scholarships and learning opportunities for people interested in politics and international relations, as well as training for people of all political stripes: libertarian/classical liberal; conservative; and progressive. These are logical on-ramps to careers in these fields.

Internships with Politicians

American Association of People with Disabilities Congressional Internship Program for Students with Disabilities

https://aapd.com/summer-internship-program

Eligible: Students with disabilities

"Each summer, since 2002, AAPD places college students, graduate students, law students, and recent graduates with all types of disabilities in summer internships with Congressional offices, federal agencies, non-profits, and for-profit organizations in the Washington, DC area."

Congressional Black Caucus

https://cbcfinc.org/internships

Eligible: Current undergraduate students who have completed a minimum of 30 credits. All students are welcome to apply regardless of race.

"CBCF's internship programs prepare college students and young professionals to become principled leaders, skilled policy analysts, and informed advocates by exposing them to the processes that develop national policies and implement them—from Capitol Hill to federal field offices."

Congressional Hispanic Caucus Internship Program

https://chci.org/programs/congressional-internship-program

Eligible: Full-time undergraduate students who are citizens of the United States

"During CHCI's paid summer and semester internships, promising Latino undergraduate students experience what it's like to work in a congressional office, while participating in weekly professional and leadership development and civic engagement through community service."

United States House of Representatives College Internships

https://house.gov/educators-and-students/college-internships

Eligible: College students

"The House offers many college internship opportunities in Washington, DC, and district offices around the U.S. Opportunities are generally available in the spring, summer, and fall. Summer positions are the most popular and most competitive. . . . Many representatives post internship information on their websites."

United States Senate Committee on Foreign Relations Internship Program

https://foreign.senate.gov/about/internships

Eligible: College students/recent graduates

"An internship with the Senate Foreign Relations Committee offers an exciting opportunity for college students, graduate students or recent graduates to gain first-hand experience working on issues of foreign policy and to learn about the legislative process."

Political Science

Atlantic Council of the United States Cyber 9/12 Student Challenge

https://atlanticcouncil.org/programs/scowcroft-center-for-strategy-and-security/cyber-statecraft-initiative/cyber-912

Eligible: Undergraduate and graduate students

"The Cyber 9/12 Strategy Challenge is an annual cyber policy and strategy competition where students from across the globe compete in developing policy recommendations tackling a fictional cyber catastrophe."

Brookings Institute Foreign Policy Program

https://brookings.edu/program/foreign-policy

Eligible: Undergraduate and graduate students

"The Foreign Policy program at Brookings is a leading center of policy-relevant scholarship exploring the rapidly re-ordering geopolitics of the great and major powers, and the disordering relations among states and transnational actors in the greater Middle East."

The Century Foundation Institute Internships

tcfinstitute.org

Eligible: Undergraduate and graduate students

"We're a progressive, nonpartisan think tank based in New York City with an additional office in Washington, D.C."

Council on Foreign Relations

https://cfr.org/academic/cfr-academic

Eligible: Undergraduate and graduate students

"The Council on Foreign Relations (CFR) is an independent, nonpartisan membership organization, think tank, and publisher dedicated to being a resource for its members, government officials, business executives, journalists, educators and students, civic and religious leaders, and other interested citizens."

Global Ties U.S.

https://globaltiesus.org/programs/emerging-leaders

Eligible: "The Emerging Leaders Program recruits standout interns and volunteers from our Network to join the National Meeting as a volunteer and participant."

"Young citizen diplomats immerse themselves in the world of public diplomacy and international exchange."

IREX (International Research & Exchanges Board)

irex.org

Eligible: Undergraduate and graduate students

"With an annual portfolio of $90 million and 400 staff worldwide, IREX works with partners in more than 100 countries in four areas essential to progress: cultivating leaders, empowering youth, strengthening institutions, and increasing access to quality education and information." For example, "Young Leaders of the Americas Initiative is an entrepreneurship-focused fellowship program for young leaders from Canada, Latin America, and the Caribbean between the ages of 25 and 35."

Naval Academy Foreign Affairs Conference

https://usna.edu/NAFAC

Eligible: College students

"Established in 1960, the Naval Academy Foreign Affairs Conference brings together more than 150 undergraduate students from the United States and over a dozen foreign countries every year for three days of critical discussions, lectures, informal exchanges, and social events."

Student Conference on United States Affairs (SCUSA) at United States Military Academy

https://usma.edu/scusa/sitepages/home.aspx

Eligible: College students with an interest in policy

"The Student Conference on U.S. Affairs is an annual four-day conference hosted by the United States Military Academy at West Point. The purpose of the conference is to facilitate interaction and constructive discussion between civilian student delegates and West Point cadets in an effort to better understand the challenges the United States faces today."

United States–Europe Relations

American Council on Germany's McCloy Fellowships

https://acgusa.org/fellowships

Eligible: Young professionals who are United States or German citizens

"The American Council on Germany's fellowships allow American and German journalists, scholars, and other mid-career professionals from a variety of fields to travel overseas to gain a better understanding of how issues are approached on the other side of the Atlantic."

American Council on Germany's Young Leaders Conference

https://acgusa.org/young-leaders

Eligible: Young leaders from a variety of industry fields who are between 28 and 38 years old

"The ACG's American-German Young Leaders Conference brings together up to 50 rising stars from government, business, journalism, academia, the military, and the non-profit sector for a week of intensive dialogue concerning domestic, bilateral, and global issues affecting both countries."

American Swiss Foundation Young Leaders Conference

https://www.americanswiss.org/members/young-leaders-conference

Eligible: Young Swiss and American individuals between the ages of 28 and 40

"Held in Switzerland each year, the conference brings together approximately 50 Americans and Swiss aged 28–40 for a week of intensive discussion and exchange on a broad range of current issues of importance to U.S.–Swiss relations; meetings with high-level diplomatic, government, business, media, and cultural leaders; and excursions to Switzerland's beautiful mountains and historic landmarks."

Asia-Europe Foundation Programs

https://asef.org/projects/themes

Eligible: Young leaders from a variety of fields

"ASEF runs more than 25 projects a year, consisting of around 100 activities, mainly conferences, seminars, workshops, lectures, publications, and online platforms, together with about 125 partner organisations."

Bucerius Summer School on Global Governance

bucerius-summer-school.de

Eligible: Young professional leaders from a variety of industries who are between 28 and 35 years of age

"The Bucerius Summer School is an annual intensive two-week summer seminar and today one of the most longstanding and successful programs of the ZEIT-Stiftung."

DAAD: German Academic Exchange Service Internship and Study Abroad Programs

daad.org

Eligible: Undergraduate and graduate students

"DAAD supports the internationalization of German universities, promotes German studies and the German language abroad, assists developing countries in establishing effective universities and advises decision makers on matters of cultural, education and development policy."

Economic Forum for Young Leaders

forum-leaders.eu

Eligible: Young leaders interested in discussing ideas and innovations concerning the future of Europe

"The biggest international social and economic meeting of young leaders in Europe."

French-American Foundation Young Leaders Program

https://frenchamerican.org/young-leaders/the-program

Eligible: Young leaders who are between 30 and 40 years of age

"The Foundation's flagship Young Leaders program was established in 1981 and has built an enduring network of leaders on both sides of the Atlantic. In this two-year program, alternating each year between France and the United States, groups of carefully selected up-and-coming leaders—in government, business, media, the military, and the cultural and non-profit sectors—spend five days discussing issues of common concern, meeting with local and global specialists, and getting to know one another."

Körber Stiftung

koerber-stiftung.de/en/

Eligible: Undergraduate and graduate students

"Körber-Stiftung takes on current social challenges in areas of activities comprising Innovation, International Dialogue and Vibrant Civil Society. At present its work focuses on three topics: Technology Needs Society, Keeping Europe Together and New Life in Exile." Among their programs: "The Munich Young Leaders programme provides a forum for future decision-makers to strengthen their international networks and inspire new thinking."

One Young World

oneyoungworld.com

Eligible: "Young leaders"

"A UK-based charity that gathers together the brightest young leaders from around the world, empowering them to make lasting connections to create positive change."

Salzburg Global Seminar

salzburgglobal.org

Eligible: Young leaders from a variety of different industry fields

"Salzburg Global convenes outstanding talent across generations, cultures and sectors to inspire new thinking and action, and to connect local innovators with global resources."

United States–Asia Relations

Asia Society—Asia 21 Young Leaders Initiative

https://asiasociety.org/asia21

Eligible: Undergraduate and graduate students

"Convenes young leaders for discussions and collaboration and unleashes them to continue working across boundaries to maximum impact."

Boao Forum for Asia

english.boaoforum.org

Eligible: Leaders who have a strong interest in issues significant to the continent of Asia

"The purpose of BFA is to . . . promote and deepen the economic exchange, coordination, and cooperation within Asia and between Asia and other parts of the world." Popularly known as the World Economic Forum (i.e. the "Davos, Switzerland") of China.

National Committee on US–China Relations Young Leaders Forum

https://ncuscr.org/ylf

Eligible: Young leaders interested in improving relations between the United States and China

"Each year, YLF holds a four-day retreat to which a select group of exceptional American and Chinese young professionals are invited."

Pacific Forum Young Leaders Program

https://pacforum.org/program/young-leaders-program

Eligible: Young professionals and graduate students between the ages of 25 and 35 who have an interest in Asia-Pacific security issues

"The Young Leaders Program was established in 2004 to enhance cross-cultural opportunities for young scholars and foreign policy professionals to improve their policy analysis skills at an early juncture in their careers."

United States–Japan Leadership Program

usjlp.org

Eligible: Young leaders from the United States and Japan who are between 28 and 42 years of age

"The purpose of the U.S.–Japan Leadership Program (USJLP) is to develop a network of communication, friendship and understanding among the next generation of leaders in each country."

Libertarian/Classical Liberal Politics

Acton Institute for the Study of Religion and Liberty

acton.org

Eligible: Undergraduate and graduate students

"The Acton Institute organizes seminars aimed at educating religious leaders of all denominations, business executives, entrepreneurs, university professors, and academic researchers in economics principles, and in the connection that can exist between virtue and economic thinking."

Cato University

Cato-university.org

Eligible: Undergraduate and graduate students

"While the topics for each Cato University program will vary, the goal remains as always: to bring together outstanding faculty and participants from across the country and, often, from around the globe, who share a commitment to liberty and learning; and to provide participants an opportunity to form new and enduring friendships and perspectives in a one-of-a-kind environment."

Foundation for Economic Education

FEE.org

Eligible: High school and college students

"The Foundation for Economic Education (FEE) is a non-political, non-profit, tax-exempt educational foundation and has been trusted by parents and teachers since 1946 to captivate and inspire tomorrow's leaders with sound economic principles and the entrepreneurial spirit."

The Independent Institute

https://independent.org/students

Eligible: High school and college students

"Our mission is to boldly advance peaceful, prosperous, and free societies grounded in a commitment to human worth and dignity."

Institute for Humane Studies

theIHS.org

Eligible: Undergraduate and graduate students

"The Institute for Humane Studies supports and partners with professors to promote the teaching and research of classical liberal ideas and to advance higher education's core purpose of intellectual discovery and human progress."

The Intercollegiate Studies Institute (ISI)

isi.org

Eligible: Undergraduate and graduate students

"Our mission: Inspiring college students to discover, embrace, and advance the principles and virtues that make America free and prosperous."

Mises Institute

mises.org

Eligible: Undergraduate and graduate students

"For scholars worldwide, the Mises Institute offers an online graduate degree program, fellowships, research grants, opportunities to publish in scholarly journals, academic conferences, access to our extensive libraries, and more."

Conservative Politics

The Fund for American Studies

tfas.org

Eligible: Undergraduate and graduate students

"Our transformational programs teach the principles of limited government, free-market economics and honorable leadership to students and young professionals in America and around the world."

Heritage Foundation Young Leaders Program

https://heritage.org/young-leaders-program

Eligible: Undergraduate and graduate students

"The Heritage Foundation Internship Program attracts young conservative leaders of the highest caliber."

Leadership Institute

leadershipinstitute.org

Eligible: Undergraduate and graduate students

"The Institute offers 47 types of training schools, workshops, and seminars; a free employment placement service; and a national field program that trains conservative students to organize campus groups."

Young America's Foundation

students.yaf.org

Eligible: High school students and college students

"Young America's Foundation is committed to ensuring that increasing numbers of young Americans understand and are inspired by the ideas of individual freedom, a strong national defense, free enterprise, and traditional values."

Young Republicans

yrnf.gop

Eligible: Undergraduate and graduate students

"Through community involvement in political issues, charitable projects and participation in political campaigns, YRs work to improve the world in which we live."

Progressive Politics

The Center on Budget and Policy Priorities

https://cbpp.org/careers/intern

Eligible: Undergraduate and graduate students

"The Center seeks highly motivated undergraduate and graduate students (including law), as well as recent graduates, . . . for full and occasionally part-time paid internships."

People for the American Way: Young People For

https://pfaw.org/young-people-for

Eligible: College students

"Young People For (YP4), a program of People For the American Way Foundation, is a national leadership development program for college-aged students that works to identify, empower, and engage the newest generation of progressive leaders."

StartingBloc

startingbloc.org

Eligible: Undergraduate and graduate students

"StartingBloc provides socially conscious students and young professionals with the training, experience, and networks necessary to drive social, economic, and environmental innovation through their careers and lives as engaged citizens."

Young Democrats of America

yda.org

Eligible: Undergraduate and graduate students

"The Young Democrats of America (YDA) is the largest youth-led, partisan political organization in the nation. The Young Democrats of America mobilizes young people under the age of 36 to participate in the electoral process to elect Democrats, influence the ideals of the Democratic Party, advocate for progressive issues, and train the next generation of progressive leaders."

18 Women, Racial Minorities, and Other Underrepresented Communities

We've listed here some selective organizations that help support women, African-American, Latino, Native American, and other groups that are often less represented in decision-making circles. These organizations offer mentoring, network-building, and in some cases financial support. We'll add that it's easier to bond with people when you have something in common.

Some of these are focused on people who are already midcareer. Even if you're still young, there's no reason you can't approach them about an internship, research project, or some other way to collaborate. It's never too early to start trying to enter a club you're excited about.

Women

Arizent Leaders

arizent.com

Arizent Leaders is "an industry-wide membership network with the focused mission of tangibly increasing gender inclusion and equality at all levels of the financial services industry."

Belizean Grove

belizeangrove.org

"The Belizean Grove is a global constellation of influential women who are key decision makers in the profit, non-profit and social sectors. . . . The Belizean Grove achieves its purpose by engaging in educational programs, mentoring programs for rising stars and giving back to our communities in the U.S. and countries we visit through vision, value and resources."

Chief

chief.com

"Chief is a private network focused on connecting and supporting women leaders. To be accepted, applicants must be C-level or a rising VP."

Women Presidents' Organization

womenpresidentsorg.com/

"The WPO is a non-profit membership organization for women presidents, CEOs, and managing directors of privately held, multimillion-dollar companies."

WomenCorporateDirectors

womencorporatedirectors.org

"WomenCorporateDirectors (WCD) is the world's largest membership organization and community of women corporate board directors."

Womensphere

womensphere.org

"Our summits and events empower our communities, develop leadership, create opportunities, and inspire impact." Offers numerous programs for students and young people.

Underrepresented Minorities

The African Middle Eastern Leadership Project

amelproject.org

"Our mission is to mobilize, empower, and unite millennial leaders and activists from the Middle East and Africa to build resilient, inclusive societies that are free from discrimination, persecution, and violent coercion, and to advocate for policies in support of these goals."

The Executive Leadership Council (ELC) Scholarship Programs

https://elcinfo.com/what-we-do/for-students

Eligible: African-American students at the undergraduate and graduate level

"The Executive Leadership Council (ELC) is the pre-eminent membership organization committed to increasing the number of global Black executives in C-Suites, on corporate boards and in global enterprises."

Harvard Arab Alumni Association World Conference

harvardarabalumni.org

Eligible: College and graduate students

"The Harvard Arab Alumni Association was founded in 2001 to promote and strengthen the 'Arab voice' at Harvard, to build a strong network among Harvard alumni with an interest in the Arab world and to provide unique fora for intelligent discussion on issues concerning the betterment of the Arab World."

INROADS Internships

Inroads.org

Eligible: Students who are from underrepresented populations and who are interested in the following fields: business, engineering, computer science, supply chain management, retail management, or health care

"For over four decades, INROADS has helped businesses gain greater access to diverse talent through continuous leadership development of outstanding ethnically diverse students and placement of those students in internships at many of North America's top corporations, firms and organizations."

Management Leadership for Tomorrow's Career Prep Program

mlt.org

Eligible: African American, Latino/Hispanic, and Native American college students

"MLT equips African Americans, Latinos and Native Americans with the skills, coaching and connections they need to lead organizations and communities worldwide."

New America Alliance

naaonline.org

Eligible: Latino and Latina leaders (membership is offered to "young leaders" who are no older than 35 years of age)

"The Alliance is organized on the principle that American Latino business leaders have a special responsibility to lead the process of building the forms of capital most crucial to Latino progress—economic capital, political capital, human capital and the practice of philanthropy."

Robert A. Toigo Foundation

toigofoundation.org

Eligible: Graduate-level students from underrepresented populations

"For 30 years, The Toigo Foundation has helped open doors for some of the most talented under-represented minorities working in the investment and finance industry today."

Seizing Every Opportunity (SEO)

seo-usa.org

Eligible: Undergraduate students from underrepresented populations

"Since 1963, SEO has made a lifetime of achievement possible for more than 14,000 talented young people from underserved and underrepresented communities around the nation."

Young Arab Leaders

yaleaders.org

Eligible: College and graduate students

"Young Arab Leaders (YAL) is an independent membership network registered as a not-for-profit business group under the Dubai Chamber. YAL empowers the next generation of leaders in the Arab World by developing a strong network of Arab industry leaders who serve as mentors to young entrepreneurs, business delegates and university students."

19 Religious Groups

You can't make a good decision about where you're going if you don't know well where you come from. Regardless of whether you call yourself profoundly religious, atheist, or just agnostic, we think there's a lot of value in learning about your heritage. At a minimum, you'll understand your family better.

We've listed here a number of impactful programs for people from some of the major faith traditions to learn more about their heritage: Christian, Jewish, and Muslim.

Christian

European Leadership Forum

euroleadership.org

Eligible: Undergraduate and graduate students

"The mission of the European Leadership Forum . . . is to unite, equip, and resource evangelical leaders to renew the biblical church and evangelise Europe."

The Zacharias Institute

https://www.rzim.org/training/zacharias-institute/about-zi

Eligible: Undergraduate and graduate students

"The Zacharias Institute is a conference center and training facility within [Ravi Zacharias International Ministries] that offers short term courses designed to instruct and equip all who desire to effectively share the gospel of Jesus Christ and answer the common objections to Christianity with gentleness and respect."

Jewish

Aish HaTorah Jerusalem Fellowships

aish.com

Eligible: Undergraduate and graduate students

"Aish HaTorah's goal is to revitalize the Jewish people by providing opportunities for Jews of all backgrounds to discover their heritage in an atmosphere of open inquiry and mutual respect."

Legacy Heritage—The Nachshon Project

https://legacyheritage.org/the-nachshon-project.html

Eligible: Jewish college students in their junior year

"The program recruits fellows (engaged college students), exposes them to innovation and excellence in leadership, to create a pool of talented, skilled and capable individuals interested in entering the field of Jewish communal work. Components of the program include: the spring semester of their junior year abroad at Hebrew University in Jerusalem."

Ohr Somayach Glassman Jewish Learning Exchange

ohr.edu

Eligible: Undergraduate and graduate male students

"The Glassman Jewish Learning Exchange was the first peer-based Jewish learning program of its kind." Based in Jerusalem.

Olami

olami.org

Eligible: Undergraduate and graduate students

"On campus, Olami identifies unaffiliated Jewish students and offers a wide-range of opportunities for student transformation and identification through text study, experiential engagement and educational trips to Israel."

ROI Community

https://schusterman.org/jewish-community-and-israel/signature-initiatives/roi-community

Eligible: Undergraduate and graduate students

"ROI Community is an international network of over 1,300 Jewish activists, entrepreneurs and innovators in their 20s and 30s who are enhancing Jewish engagement and fostering positive social change globally."

Taglit-Birthright Israel

birthrightisrael.com

Eligible: Undergraduate and graduate students

"Birthright Israel seeks to ensure the future of the Jewish people by strengthening Jewish identity, Jewish communities, and connection with Israel via a trip to Israel for the majority of Jewish young adults from around the world."

Tikvah Fund

tikvahfund.org

Eligible: Undergraduate and graduate students

"The Tikvah Fund is a philanthropic foundation and ideas institution committed to supporting the intellectual, religious, and political leaders of the Jewish people and the Jewish State."

Muslim

Muslim American Leadership Alliance

malanational.org/about

"The MALA Young Leaders Fellowship is a MALA initiative to provide leadership development and civic engagement opportunities for young Muslim Americans."

20 Mini-Universities: Conferences and Communities for Further Learning

We've listed here some of the conferences and places for further learning where leaders from many sectors of society meet one another. Some of these programs have very strict application criteria, which unsurprisingly means that the people who get in tend to be particularly accomplished. These all offer you the ability to meet some of the most accomplished people in your industry.

We've also listed a number of programs that are the functional equivalent of a graduate degree or certificate, for less money and less time. These are selective learning programs that will grant you unique skills and a powerful network.

Selective Conferences and Communities

Clinton Global Initiative

https://clintonfoundation.org/clinton-global-initiative

Eligible: Students and leaders who are interested in addressing significant global issues

"The Clinton Global Initiative (CGI) convenes leaders from across sectors to drive action through its unique model. Rather than directly implementing projects, CGI facilitates action by helping members connect, collaborate, and develop Commitments to Action which are new, specific, and measurable plans that address global challenges."

The Feast

feastongood.com

Eligible: Leaders and innovators from across different sectors of society

"By hosting a Feast dinner, we not only delight in each other, we change the world; one dinner, one conversation, one connection at a time."

Renaissance Weekends

RenaissanceWeekend.org

Eligible: Interesting people

"Incredible mix of preeminent leaders, passionate change-makers and rising stars of all ages. More than a conference: invitation-only, off-the-record. Non-partisan: All participants heard, all opinions welcome. More light than heat."

Singularity University Programs

singularityu.org

Eligible: Business professionals and leaders

"Singularity University is a global learning and innovation community using exponential technologies to tackle the world's biggest challenges . . . We offer educational programs, courses, and summits; enterprise strategy, leadership, and innovation programs; programs to support and scale startups and promote social impact; and online news and content."

Technology Entertainment Design (TED)

Ted.com

Eligible: Anyone who can pay (scholarships available)

"TED is a nonprofit devoted to spreading ideas, usually in the form of short, powerful talks (18 minutes or less). TED began in 1984 as a conference where Technology, Entertainment and Design converged, and today covers almost all topics—from science to business to global issues—in more than 110 languages."

World Academy of Art and Science

worldacademy.org

Eligible: College and graduate students

"The Academy serves as a forum for reflective scientists, artists, and scholars dedicated to addressing the pressing challenges confronting humanity today independent of political boundaries or limits, whether spiritual or physical."

YEC Young Entrepreneur Council

yec.co

An "invitation-only forum to exchange ideas and resources, make high-value connections and provide needed mentorship . . . 'The most elite entrepreneurship organization in America'—to date, the invite-only organization has accepted less than 10 percent of the over 14,000 applications."

Short-Term Learning Programs for Midcareer Professionals

We've listed here some programs that typically require more of a long-term commitment than just attending a several-day conference. They also in most cases have a very significant application process, comparable to applying for a graduate degree.

Aspen Institute: Civil Society Fellowship

civilsocietyfellowship.org

Eligible: "Between the ages of 25 and 45"

The Anti-Defamation League "and the Aspen Institute have launched the Civil Society Fellowship . . . modeled on the Henry Crown Fellowship [also profiled in this chapter]."

Aspen Institute: Henry Crown Fellowship

https://aspeninstitute.org/leadership-programs/henry-crown-fellowship-program

Eligible: High-achieving entrepreneurial leaders who are between 30 and 45 years of age

"The Henry Crown Fellowship Program . . . seeks to develop the next generation of community-spirited leaders . . . Each year, a class of 20–22 leaders is chosen to engage in a thought-provoking journey of personal exploration."

Aspen Institute: Socrates Program

https://aspeninstitute.org/programs/socrates-program

Eligible: Upcoming leaders in various industries

"The Aspen Institute Socrates Program provides a forum for emerging leaders from various professions to convene and explore contemporary issues through expert-moderated dialogue."

Coro Fellows Programs

coro.org

Eligible: Individuals who have just earned their undergraduate and graduate degrees as well as young professionals

"During this nine-month program, each Fellow participates in a series of full-time projects across a variety of sectors in public affairs, including a final independent project of the Fellow's choosing."

Harvard Business School Young American Leaders Program

hbs.edu

"The Young American Leaders Program model at HBS is designed to help local leaders in urban areas create locally-based solutions for shared prosperity."

Iacocca Global Village at Lehigh University

https://global.lehigh.edu/iacocca/globalvillage

Eligible: Young professionals as well as undergraduate and graduate students

"The Iacocca Global Village for Future Leaders is an intensive, five-week leadership experience at Lehigh University that helps you build cross-cultural leadership, professional, business and entrepreneurship skills, preparing you to thrive in a global community."

Organization for Youth Education and Development Young Leaders' Forums

https://www.oyed.org/index.php?en_ylf

Eligible: Young leaders who have an interest in one of the given conference topics

"Over the last decade we have developed a broad range of forums focusing on diverse bi- and multi-lateral relationships within and between Africa, Asia, Europe, North and South America."

Presidential Leadership Scholars

presidentialleadershipscholars.org

"Each year, a diverse group of mid-career professionals begin a journey to hone their leadership abilities through interactions with former presidents, key administration officials, leading academics, and business and civic leaders."

White House Fellowships

https://whitehouse.gov/get-involved/fellows

Eligible: Young professionals who have received their undergraduate degree and are citizens of the United States

"Selected individuals typically spend a year working as a full-time, paid Fellow to senior White House Staff, Cabinet Secretaries and other top-ranking government officials. Fellows also participate in an education program consisting of roundtable discussions with leaders from the private and public sectors, and trips to study U.S. policy in action both domestically and internationally."

World Economic Forum of Young Global Leaders

younggloballeaders.org

"The Forum of Young Global Leaders is a community with the vision, courage and influence to drive positive change." Popularly known as the Davos YGLs.

What Happens Next?

Every book on success says the secret to success is "hard work." Well . . . that's not exactly true. **The secret to success is hard work, applied in the right direction.** What we've tried to do is provide you with ideas and suggestions for maximizing your educational experience and first few jobs in your career. If you choose the right activities, and apply the right effort, then you too can maximize the return on your education.

That said, we can't possibly cover all relevant resources. We strongly recommend you look on Google or another Internet search engine for all combinations of words from each of the two columns on the right in the table, for example, "physics young leaders" or "computer science internships." This will surface more opportunities that want to give you money, attention, and access.

Category	Your personal keywords	What you're seeking
Field of study	"computer science"	**Learning**: "education," "fellowship," "scholarship"
Location, either your hometown or where you live now	"New York"	
Target industry or job title	"fashion," "doctor"	**Community**: "alliance," "association," "community," "conference," "council," "forum," "institute," "network," "organization," "retreat," "society," "symposium"
Your high school, college, or other educational institution	"Branson High School"	
Hobbies/extracurriculars/interests	"Track and field"	**Early-career peers**: "leadership development," "mentors," "young," "young leaders"
Nationality	"American"	
Religion	"Jewish"	
Race	"African-American" or "Black"	**Jobs:** "career," "internships"

George Bernard Shaw famously said, "Youth is wasted on the young." We want to make sure you take full advantage of your #1 asset, your youth.

We'd love your feedback on our book. In particular, we keep a database of acceleration programs for ambitious young people, like the ones we have highlighted here. If you have any you'd like to add, please contact either of us via our websites (see the following links) and we may include it in the next edition of the book. We're excited to hear about the impact we've had on your life and career. Good luck!

Mandee Heller Adler, `InternationalCollegeCounselors.com`, `EditTheWork.com`

David Teten, `Teten.com`, `VersatileVC.com`

Acknowledgments

From both of us: A special shout out to the team at Wiley-Amy Fandrei, Mackenzie Thompson, Pete Gaughan, Georgette Beatty and Richard Marshall-for embracing this book, and for helping it become a reality.

Manddee: My humblest gratitude goes out to my unparalleled mother and sisters, Beverly Heller, Aimee Heller and Cheree Heller Liebowitz, for all their work and support. I can feel dad smiling each time we work together. I would also like to thank the brilliant marketing, editing, and writing experts at International College Counselors, including my business partner, Barry Liebowitz. Finally, I am so thankful for the thousands of students who have welcomed me as a mentor and college counselor. Your success makes me so proud. Keep aiming high!

David: Many people have reviewed past blog posts, emails, and other content that has been absorbed into this book. Thank you to David Alworth, Justine Chan, Akshat Dixit, David Frankel, Prabhat Gusain Taimur Hassan, Katherine Boe Heuck, Aishwarya Iyer, Matt Joyce, Sandra Kerka, Janet Kwok, Aleksandra Mikhaylova, Navid Nathoo, Mimi Owusu, Raphaela Sapire, Paulina Symala, Leona Teten, and Joan Xie, among others. It took a village and two decades to research and then eventually help aggregate dozens of emails, blog posts, and essays that I have written into this book. Georgette Beatty of Wiley was exceptionally thorough in her review.

I really wrote this book for my children, and I appreciate them intermittently giving me some quiet time to write it. I hope they—and you—read it thoroughly and take a lot of value from it. I am eternally grateful to my wife for our children, who are only a small fraction of her many contributions to our shared life. I am honored to dedicate the book to my father Jean, who passed away in the last stages of writing this book. I owe him for everything.

Endnotes

1. David Teten is an investor via HOF Capital.
2. Brendan Dowling, "I Graduated from the Library: An Interview with Ray Bradbury," *Public Libraries*, Nov/Dec 2002, https://publiclibrariesonline.org/2013/05/i-graduated-from-the-library-an-interview-with-ray-bradbury/.
3. Brandon Busteed and Zac Auter, "Career-Relevant Education Linked to Student Well-Being," Gallup, February 13, 2018, https://news.gallup.com/opinion/gallup/226934/career-relevant-education-linked-student.aspx.
4. Reid Hoffman, "My 2020 Vision," https://linkedin.com/pulse/my-2020-vision-graduates-how-optimistic-terrible-times-reid-hoffman/?mc_cid=79ca033fd6&mc_eid=9b22fa87eb.
5. This section is adapted from the book *The Virtual Handshake: Opening Doors and Closing Deals Online* by David Teten and Scott Allen; learn more at https://teten.com/tvh.
6. Jodi Kantor, "At Harvard, a Master's in Problem Solving," *New York Times*, December 24, 2011, https://nytimes.com/2011/12/25/us/politics/how-harvard-shaped-mitt-romney.html.
7. Frank Bruni, "How to Get the Most Out of College," *New York Times*, August 17, 2018, https://nytimes.com/2018/08/17/opinion/college-students.html.
8. https://asktheharvardmba.com/2009/04/12/what-do-you-wish-someone-had-told-you-before-starting-hbs/, downloaded June 14, 2009 (site no longer active).
9. David Teten is an investor via HOF Capital.
10. Noah Zandan and Hallie Lynch, "Dress for the (Remote) Job You Want," *Harvard Business Review*, June 18, 2020, https://hbr.org/2020/06/dress-for-the-remote-job-you-want.

11. This section draws in part on Art Markman, "How to Become Friends with Your Coworkers While Working Remotely," Fast Company, July 16, 2020, https://fastcompany.com/90516285/how-to-become-friends-with-your-coworkers-while-working-remotely.
12. David Teten, "On Structural Holes in Your Business Relationships," November 6, 2004, https://teten.com/blog/2004/06/11/on-structural-holes-in-your-business-relationships.
13. Page 1 of the 1996 Harvard Business School MBA Program brochure.
14. Leadership IQ, "Leadership IQ Study: Why New Hires Fail," September 20, 2005, https://prweb.com/releases/2005/09/prweb287275.htm.

Index

A

B

D

E

F